NOAH'S FLOOD

WHEN WHERE WHY
THE CONCLUSIVE EVIDENCE

NOAH'S FLOOD

WHEN WHERE WHY
THE CONCLUSIVE EVIDENCE

Walter Parks

UnKnownTruths.com
Publishing Company

Orlando, Florida

UNKNOWNTRUTHS.COM
PUBLISHING COMPANY
8815 Conroy Windermere Rd. Ste 190
Orlando, FL 32835

www.unknowntruths.com

Printed in Canada

Illustrations and Layout by Dan Diehl

Library of Congress Control Number (LCCN): 2003096659

UNKNOWNTRUTHS.COM
PUBLISHING COMPANY

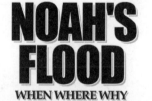

**NOAH'S
FLOOD**
WHEN WHERE WHY
THE CONCLUSIVE EVIDENCE

By Walter Parks

Includes bibliographical references and index.

ISBN 0-9745393-0-9

About

UnKnownTruths.com
Publishing Company

UnKnownTruths.com Publishing Company was formed to publish true stories of the unusual or of the previously unexplained. These stories will typically provide radically different views from those that have shaped the understandings of our natural world, our religions, our science, our history, and even the foundations of our civilizations.

The Company's stories will also include stories of the very important life-extending medical breakthroughs; stem cell therapies; genetic therapies; cloning and other emerging findings that promise to change the very meaning of life.

Each story will depict important and interesting artifacts, photographs, paintings, and other art objects. Replicas of these artifacts and art objects will be available as souvenirs and **Collectible Historical Artifacts**™, or in the case of more modern stories, such "artifacts" and art objects will be available as souvenirs and **Collectible Future Artifacts**™.

These collectibles will be available from:

UnKnownTruths.com
Publishing Company

v

Dedication

This book is dedicated to my nephew and key researcher, Stephen Ragsdale. Steve, as an outstanding history teacher, used his great knowledge to help me find the ancient keys to break the code that reinterprets the seemingly unrelated **evidence that proves the validity of the true story of Noah's Flood.**

Figure 1: Noah's Flood

Contents

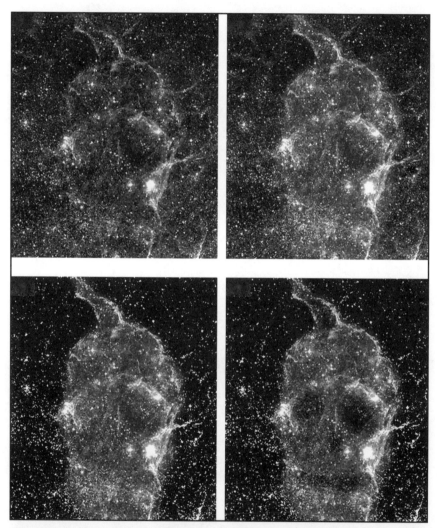

Figure 2: The upper left is an actual photograph of the real Satan as he appears today. The other three are computer enhanced to help visualize the Satan that caused Noah's Flood.

Illustrations

Acknowledgements

"History is the version of past events that people have decided to agree upon."

Napoleon Bonaparte
1769 - 1821

In writing this book, I stood on the shoulders of giants. Most of the concepts and material herein is based on ancient documents written by great, unknown authors in the era we have previously called pre-history.

Pre-history because most of today's professional historians in academia have not yet recognized the great antiquity of some of the stories in the clay tablets of ancient Babylon and Sumer, nor the even greater age of some parts of the Hebrew Bible. Nor has academia recognized the great antiquity of some pre-history civilizations.

But the evidence is conclusive that great civilizations did exist more than 11,000 years ago. It is hoped that academia will soon acknowledge this certain fact.

I am deeply grateful to the unknown writers of yesteryear for providing me the insight to this certain fact.

I am also deeply indebted to the great classical writers of a much later age. The principal ones are Homer writing in about 800 BC, Herodotus in about 450 BC, Plato about 380 BC, Strabo about 30 BC, and Ovid in 1 AD. They had access to ancient documents and oral traditions that are not available today. Yet we can see elements from their source stories when we carefully study their writings and compare such elements that are common among them.

Extracting these common elements and comparing them to similar elements from the stories in the clay tablets and the other sources from greater antiquity, established the foundation for this book.

The story that developed from this foundation was very

adverse to the established understandings of human history and religion. It therefore had to be verified by scientific evidence to have any credibility.

I am grateful to a more modern group of writers for providing insight to existing scientific data. These writers include I. Donnelly writing in 1882 and 1885, R. B. Anderson in 1888, I. Velikovsky in 1956 and 1977, C. H. Hapgood in 1958 through 1979, G. Hawkins in 1977, C. Sagan in 1977, J. A. West in 1979 and 1989, Z. Sitchin in 1983 and 1990, G. Hancock in 1993, R. Bauval in 1994, C. Wilson in 1995, Rand and Rose Flem-Ath in 1995, D. S. Allan and J. B. Delair in 1997.

I cannot agree with all the conclusions of these modern writers in that the evidence for some of their ideas is not as conclusive for me. The evidence does, however, support some of my ideas, and I am grateful to them for the insights their work provided.

The unknown writers of old; the classical writers of ancient Greece and Rome; and the modern writers listed above, all shaped my understandings of, arguably, the greatest event in the history of mankind.

The generally unknown truths revealed by these ancient stories and contemporary scientific evidence is fundamental to our understanding of true history, important to some of our religious concepts, and vital to foretelling our future - and the destiny of mankind.

I thank them all.

Preface

Please read this.

Truth that is unknown by the reader - no matter how well written, or how poorly written - will be altered by the reader.

Truth will be altered because of the biases shaped by the reader's background and experiences; by his or her education and ethics; and by his or her religious beliefs.

Great truthful documents of the past have been so altered. We need to understand this as we try to interpret such documents - and, of course - our interpretation will further alter the original.

Fiction, however, can be read with a willingness to suspend reality. The biases are then not nearly so dominating. The mind can be more open, more receptive.

Please read this book as a work of fiction, especially so in the parts derived from ancient "myths". And some of the book is fiction in that I have "enhanced" the story in the places of transitions between available facts.

But I must warn you, buried within is a great truth, a largely unknown truth.

How well you suspend reality, and how dominating your biases may be, will determine how much of the great truth you see.

In any event...

Enjoy,
Walter Parks

Sumerian Cuniform

Egyptian Hyrogliphics

Indian SanScript (Punjabi)
ਸਅਟਅਨ ਕਅਉਸਬਦ ਟਹਏ ਫਲਉੳਦ

Aramaic

Hebrew
דוֹולֹט דֹהת דֹדֹסעאאש נאתאס

English
Satan caused the flood.

Figure 3: Satan caused the flood.

Chapter I
Introduction

Definition of a Myth:

"A traditional story originating in a pre-literate society, dealing with supernatural beings, ancestors, or heroes that serve as primordial types in a primitive view of the world."
The American Heritage Dictionary

The myth of Noah's Flood was based on fact.
It really did happen.
The entire Earth was covered with waters that destroyed almost all life on Earth.

I grew up being taught to believe in the literal word of the Bible. As I got older and went off to college, I learned that there was simply not enough water on Earth to cover the entire land in a great flood.

I therefore rationalized that even if the Bible were true, it is not literal. Perhaps only a local flood wiped out the life in the area where the old Patriarchs lived.

But then I learned that there were many stories of a great flood that covered the entire world. The stories came from almost all parts of the world. Even then I rationalized that maybe people from the area of the flood migrated to new lands and took their stories with them.

I just could not believe that such a flood really happened.

But all through life, I kept hearing of the Great Flood.

I had to find the truth.

I searched the ancient documents and legends. I studied the related "myths". I searched for ancient artifacts. I searched for any scientific evidence.

I found the truth.

There really was a worldwide flood. The evidence is conclusive.

The ancient literature provides the basic story, but has been contaminated down through the ages with revisions and additions that distort the facts. But the reason for the changes and the resulting distortions become clear when all the facts are considered.

Scientific evidence was found to be more conclusive, but lacks the color of the myths. But when properly combined with the "myths", the scientific facts take on the glow of the ancient literature and the deep meanings of ancient traditions. And the truths come shinning through.

The result is a wonderful understanding of ancient truths. The ancient unknown truths become clear, and even more colorful than any of the great legends and myths that derived from the truths.

Perhaps the best way to tell the story is to describe it in terms of what the ancients believed that they witnessed. We will then trace the evolution of their eyewitness stories, down through the ages, to see how the many legends, myths, and stories developed.

We will also describe the actual events in terms of available scientific evidence.

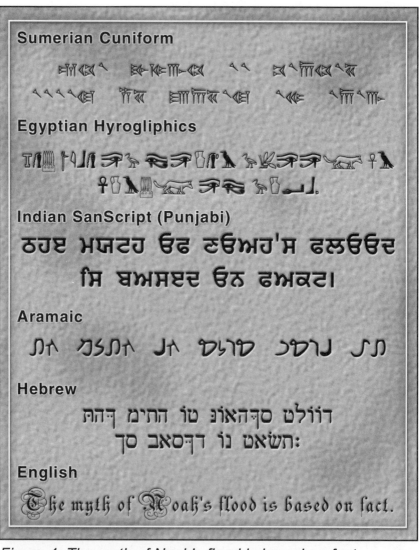

Figure 4: The myth of Noah's flood is based on fact.

The weaving of science, history, myths, and legends will result in a clear and colorful understanding of perhaps the greatest event in the history of mankind.

Let's first use the ancient literature to help us imagine how it all began - in the eyes and minds of the people that actually witnessed the great disaster.

Factual data will be used to the extent of its availability. Voids between the factual data will be filled with suppositions suggested by the body of information.

The names will be the actual people named in the ancient literature.

We will consider the ancient stories from the earliest writings of mankind.

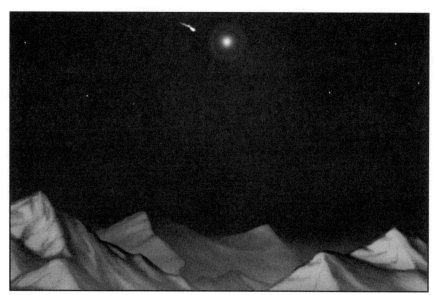

Figure 5: Eliphaz saw Satan thrown out of the Heavens.

Figure 6: The interpretation down thru the ages.

Chapter 2
The Warning

The God Enki warned Ziusudra, King of Shuruppak that the Gods were going to destroy mankind with a great flood.
Summerian Clay Tablet

The God EA warned King Uthnapishtem that the Gods were going to destroy mankind with a great flood.
Akkadian Clay Tablet

God tells Noah to **"Make thee an ark..."** *so he and his family can survive a great flood that God plans to send to destroy mankind.*
The Book of Genesis

Atlantis: April 1, 9619 BC

Eliphaz knew more about the gods than any other holy man in Atlantis. He had been watching them in the night skies all his life.

No wonder he was the first to see Satan thrown out of heaven.

He first saw Satan being hurled to earth when Satan, falling from the upper heavens, passed the great god Neptune. He started spitting fire at Neptune. Eliphaz could see the fire in the clear night sky.

That made Neptune mad. He threw a large bolt of lighting at Satan. It made Satan quit spitting fire, but Satan still glowed red hot in anger as he fell past Neptune.

Eliphaz watched all night. Eventually Satan's anger lessened and he didn't glow so bright. Finally he was too dim for Eliphaz to see him in the brightening morning sky.

Eliphaz wondered what Satan had done to make the gods throw him out of heaven. He wondered what Satan would do when he landed on earth.

He better go tell the king that Satan was coming.

Eliphaz waited until the King was ready to receive his chief priest. Sometimes the king maintained his privacy until late in the morning.

Finally Eliphaz was lead before King Atlas the VII. Atlas was a very old man, but he spoke with the charisma, strength, and twinkling eyes of a confident, much younger man.

Atlas
Good morning Eliphaz. Have you had your breakfast?

Eliphaz
No sir. I have been waiting to see you.

Atlas smiles at the mild rebuff. He then studies his priest for a moment and sees his great concern. Atlas motions for a servant to bring in food and drink, and motions for Eliphaz to take a seat at a large, but low table.

Atlas
Is there a problem?

Eliphaz
Sire, there has been an argument
in heaven. The gods have thrown
one of their own out of heaven.

Atlas has a mixture of amusement and concern. He frowns and takes a drink from his morning juice.

Atlas
How do you know this? Did you
have a dream? A vision?

Eliphaz
I saw it with my own eyes.

Atlas is surprised. He takes a bite of food and studies his chief priest for a long moment, and then gestures for Eliphaz to continue.

Eliphaz
Sire, you know that the gods normally
stay in heaven. Each patrols his own
area and we have studied their actions
for many, many generations.

Atlas
Yes?

Eliphaz

Every time something happens in heaven, it affects our lives here on earth.

Atlas

Yes. Yes it does.

Eliphaz

Last night, the gods threw one of their own out of heaven. I saw him fight with the great god Neptune.

Atlas

And who is this god they threw out?

Eliphaz

I do not know him. I have never seen him. I call him Satan.

Atlas

You call him…. Satan?

Eliphaz

Yes sir. He looked like a great serpent when he passed Neptune. And if he angered the other gods, he must be evil. I named him Satan because that means evil serpent.

Atlas

I see. Where did he land?

Eliphaz

I do not know. Ra, the great day god (the sun) started the day before he landed. I could only see him in the night.

Atlas

What should we do?

Eliphaz

I do not know great King.

Atlas

Shall I call the homeland army to assemble?

Eliphaz

To fight a god?

Atlas

To fight anyone, anything that threatens Atlantis!

Eliphaz

Yes sir.

Atlas turns to a servant.

Atlas

Have Merlota call my generals.

Eliphaz becomes afraid that he may have given an unwarranted alarm.

Eliphaz

Sire…. He may not have yet
landed. Last night, he was falling
very slowly…. And…. It is a long
way from heaven to earth.

Atlas

I will be ready for him…. Whenever
he gets here.

Atlas paces the floor.

Atlas

What does he want? What will he do?

Eliphaz

I do not know Sire…. But if he has
lost his kingdom in heaven, he may
want one here on earth.

Atlas

Mine?

Eliphaz

Sire. Yours is the greatest.

The King paces and thinks.

Atlas

We must find him. Destroy him!

Eliphaz

Destroy a god?!!

Atlas

Yes!

Eliphaz is appalled.

Eliphaz

Sire. Please…. Do not say such
things. The gods could strike you
down!

Atlas becomes demanding, almost threatening.

Atlas

You speak to the other gods. I am
their ally against this…. This Satan!
Together we can defeat him.

Eliphaz

Yes sire. I will go pray…. And offer
a…. a sacred bull.

Atlas

Yes!

Eliphaz

The white bull.

Atlas

My prize bull?

Eliphaz

For the alliance with the gods.

Atlas

Yes. For the alliance.

Eliphaz bows and hurries away. Atlas thinks for a long moment and then walks out on his balcony and looks to the sun in heaven.

Atlas
Oh greatest God, King of all gods.
I, Atlas, King of all men, am at your
service. I know that this Satan must
have offended you for you to have
banned him from heaven. He is your
enemy, therefore he is my enemy.
Tell me what to do to destroy him!

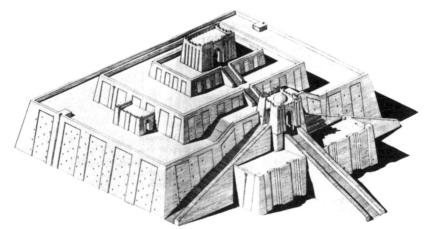

Figure 7: The Mesopotamians observed the heavens from atop the Ziggurat.

Figure 8: Semiramis is in awe of Marduk's approach.

Mesopotamia: April 1, 9619 BC

Nimrod the First was the King of all of ancient Mesopotamia. He had proclaimed himself a god, and he had made his beautiful wife, Semiramis, the "Queen of Heaven". He had made his people stop worshipping the popular god Tiamat, and worship Semiramis instead.

He had built the great observatory for the study of the gods in heaven. He knew that he would one day go there. And he did. He died and became a god in Heaven.

He promised Semiramis that he would be in touch with her just as soon as he could. He left Semiramis and their son, Tammuz, in charge.

Semiramis had watched the skies, searching for some sign of Nimrod, ever night since his death.

Then it happened, the priests called Semiramis up on the great Ziggurat to witness the fight between Neptune and a new god.

The bright glow, and mighty lighting bolts from this new god entranced her. Could it be Nimrod?
It must be. He was coming to earth. She could see that. He must be coming to see her!

She became excited!

She was disappointed when the morning light made the new god invisible.

But she was there the next night. And so was the new god. He was getting closer.

She watched night after night. He got closer each night. She remembered something that Nimrod had said; about planning to make changes in heaven. He said he would become "Marduk", which meant rebel in the language of ancient Babylon. She almost giggled at the realization.

Nimrod was now the god Marduk, and he was coming to see her!

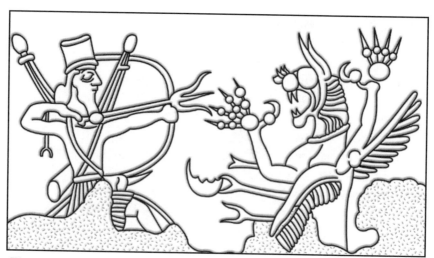

Figure 9: Marduk battles Tiamat.

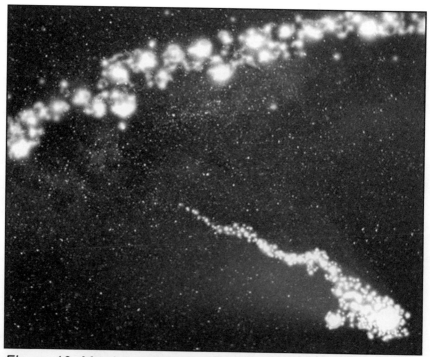

Figure 10: Marduk blasts Tiamat into millions of pieces to form the "hammered necklace" mentioned in the Bible.

Suddenly the god Tiamat threw a great tongue of fire at Marduk. Semiramis became alarmed! This proved to her that Marduk was Nimrod. She and Nimrod had always opposed the goddess Tiamat. Nimrod had made his people stop worshipping Tiamat and to worship her, Semiramis instead - as the earth mother god, and the Queen of Heaven.

Tiamat was trying to stop Marduk from coming to earth!

But Marduk was determined. He headed straight for Tiamat.

Impact!

Marduk shattered Tiamat into thousands of pieces, amid a great, fiery explosion.

Semiramis became concerned.

The pieces of Tiamat spread out into a glowing necklace of fiery beads. And Marduk came flying out of the great balls of fire.

Semiramis' concern developed into another smile. Yes, he was coming to see her. Nimrod knew how much she loved necklaces. He had torn her enemy Tiamat apart and made a necklace in the night sky - just for her!

Figure 11: "It is so hard to understand gods."

Western North America: April 17, 9619 BC

    Ta-Wats the hare trapper was up early that morning so he could get to his traps before the birds and other animals found his catches. He saw the great collision of the stars. He stared in fascination. What in the world are the gods in heaven doing now?

    It is so hard to understand gods.

    He watched until the rising sun made the stars too dim to see. He shook his head in his lack of understanding, and hurried to his traps.

    The next morning he again got up before the sun, to check his traps. He looked up at the stars, where he had seen the collision the previous night.

    The colliding stars seemed to be falling to earth. What in the world knocked them out of heaven? He had seen shooting stars, and falling stars before. But this one was much bigger than he had ever seen before. He watched to see where it would fall.

    But the morning sun came and blotted out Ta-Wats' view.

    Oh well. He better get to his traps.

    Morning after morning he watched the stars as they kept falling towards earth. They kept getting bigger and bigger.

    After a few days, he could still see them even when the sun came up. These are no ordinary shooting stars!

    He ignored his traps and watched the approaching balls of fire.

Atlantis: April 18, 9619 BC

Eliphaz is ushered into the presence of King Atlas. He is carrying an arm full of scrolls.

Atlas
What have you learned?

Eliphaz
Great King, I have searched the ancient records.

Atlas
And?

Figure 12: "The gods have given us a warning."

Eliphaz

In the past…. It is recorded that much of this great land was destroyed by earthquakes and floods.

Atlas

What lands?

Eliphaz

Atlantis was a much larger continent 18,500 years ago. There was a disturbance in heaven. It caused problems here.

Atlas

Yes, you said earlier that every time something happens in heaven, that it affects our lives here on earth.

Eliphaz

Yes. The records show that….

Atlas

First, tell me what we need to do.

Eliphaz

The gods have given us a warning. We need to prepare….

Atlas

Prepare for what?

Eliphaz

Another destruction…. Another great flood.

Atlas

Flood?

Eliphaz

Yes. All the lands will be flooded.
All the way up most mountains.

Atlas

Are you sure?

Eliphaz holds up the ancient scrolls.

Eliphaz

This is our warning. We must
accept this warning from the gods.
We must…. Prepare.

Atlas

Prepare for a flood?

Eliphaz

Yes. A very great flood.

Atlas

I have 1200 ships. We could
put some of our people on the ships.
They will float above a flood.

Eliphaz

Yes…. But there will be great
waves.

Atlas

My ships are strong.

Eliphaz

Yes. Put our people in them.
But, sire…. May I suggest that you….
You must survive. It may be safer
in the high mountains.

Atlas studies his chief priest.

Atlas

You are asking me to take great
measures.

Eliphaz

Sire…. These are perilous times.

There is a long moment of silence.

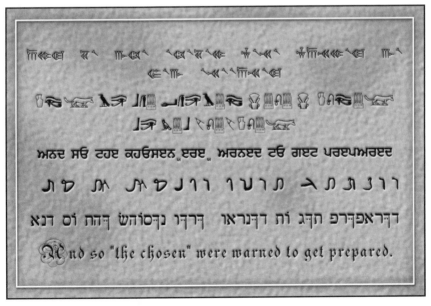

Figure 13

Atlas
I'll order that the boats be filled.

Eliphaz
And you will go to the mountains?

Atlas again studies his chief priest.

Atlas
Gather our most learned. We will
go to my son's home. He lives
near the top of our highest mountain.

Eliphaz
Yes, Mount Meru. I shall prepare.

Eliphaz bows to Atlas, and hurries out.

The surviving Atlantians were dispersed and later migrated to all the populated lands of earth. There were also non-Atlantian survivors that mixed with the Atlantian survivors in these shared lands.

The stories of the warning, as experienced by the various survivors, were retold generation after generation. And with each retelling they changed - bit by bit.

Figure 14: Artifacts recounting the adventures of Gilgamesh.

Figure 15: Ziusudra is warned by the god Enki through a reed wall to build a large ship to escape a flood that the other gods are sending to destroy mankind because the people are not serving the gods.

Epic of Gilgamesh - Sumerian Version

Most scholars recognize the Epic of Gilgamesh as the oldest of these stories.

In ancient times, King Ashurbanipal of Assyria had a library at Ninevah. Archeologists excavated it and were able in 1872 to read some of the clay tablets found there.

The story on these clay tablets was later traced back to an almost identical Sumerian story found on tablet fragments dating back to about 3,000 BC. Evidence indicates that the story was copied at that time from much more ancient writings.

The tablets say that the god Enki warned Ziusudra, the King of Shuruppak, that the gods were going to destroy mankind with a great flood. Details of the story are presented in Chapter Seven.

Akkadian Version

The clay tablets of later years tell an almost identical story of the warning, except the god Ea gives the warning to King Uthnapishtim (or Utnaphistum) of Shuruppak.

Ea stands by the wall of the house of Uthnapishtim and tells him about the decision of the gods to cause a flood and that he should build a ship to save himself. The details are also given in Chapter Seven.

Figure 16: At God's instructions, Noah builds an ark.

Biblical Version

The most well known story of the flood is, of course, that of Noah as told in the King James version of the Bible. It is very similar to the Sumerian and Babylonian stories, except the one true God - Jehovah - gives the warning to Noah, who is one of the patriarchs in the Bible.

God decides to destroy all mankind.

"But Noah found grace in the eyes of the Lord."
Genesis 6:8

So God decides to save Noah and tells him to build an ark.

"Make thee an ark of gopher wood; ..."
Genesis 6:14

Noah did, and then God sent the flood.

"... all the fountains of the deep (were) broken up, and the windows of heaven were opened."
Genesis 7:11

(Note the phrase "fountains of the deep", perhaps implying more than rain. It is usually taught that the flood was caused by rain.)

So Noah and his family are saved.

It seems clear that the Hebrews either copied and modified their story from the very much earlier story of Ziusudra, or that both stories came from a common, earlier source. More is described on this possibility in Chapter Seven.

Greek "Myth"

The so called Greek myths tell a similar story of the warning, except in them, Prometheus, described as a wise benefactor of humanity (a priest?) and the father of Deucalion, King of Phthia in Thessaly (Thessalia), gives the warning to Deucalion, who then builds a "chest" in which his family floats and survives the flood.

It is interesting to note that Deucalion means "new-wine sailor". This may refer to Deucalion having been a "maritime person", perhaps even an Atlantian. The Bible also refers to Noah as a maritime person.

Egyptian Version

In the Egyptian version of the flood story, there is no warning.

American Indian (Ute) Version

In the Ute "legends", they see something approaching, but do not understand it, nor do they perceive it as a warning.

The Key Flood Stories

Country	Warned By	Why	Hero
Sumer	Enki	Not serving gods	Ziusudra
Akkadian	Ea	Not serving gods	Uthnapishtim
Greece	Prometheus	Wickedness	Deucalion
Hebrew	Jehovah	Wickedness	Noah
Ute	No one	None	Ta-Wats
Norse			Thor
Persia	Gods		Yima
Egypt	No one	None	Osiris

Figure 17: God gave warnings.

Warning Summary

There are several other stories of the flood - all with different names and places, apparently re-written from earlier versions when names of people and places were changed to be recognizable by the writers of the time. Old names of people and places destroyed in the flood - and written in foreign languages, "needed" to be made understandable.

But the stories clearly imply that God gave the warnings to:

1. Eliphaz, Chief Priest of Atlantis;
2. Ziusudra, King of Shuruppak;
3. Uthnapishtim, King of Shuruppak;
4. Deucalion, King of Phthia; and
5. Noah, of the Hebrew Bible.

And it may well be that all of these are variations of a single story: the story of Eliphaz of Atlantis, as evidence to be presented later suggests.

There were also those that saw Satan coming, but did not understand it as a warning. The Egyptian version falls into this category, as does the Ta-Wats American Indian version. All of these stories, and other flood stories are expanded in Chapter Seven.

Figure 18: Satan, the great dragon, comes to Earth.

Chapter 3
Satan Comes to Earth

"And there was a war in heaven;
... and the great dragon was cast out, that old
serpent called the Devil and Satan ...
*   Revelation 12:7-9*

Witnesses from many ancient cultures observed and recorded seeing Satan come to Earth.

Figure 19: King Atlas and his group watch as Satan and his demons approach earth.

Mount Meru: May 5, 9619

King Atlas and his entourage fled to the home of his
son who lived in the mountains. There they watched Satan
fall to earth. He was now very large and could be seen
even in full daylight. He was almost as bright as the sun.
He looked like a great, twisting, fiery serpent.
Atlas turns to Eliphaz.

Atlas
Satan is indeed a fitting name.

They watch as the great winds rise to meet Satan.
They watch as earth and Satan exchange great bolts of
lighting.
And Satan keeps coming.
One of Satan's assistants comes closest.
Suddenly the assistant explodes into millions of pieces
of fiery demigods. Many plunged to earth. Many returned
to heaven, many stayed with Satan.
Then Satan and most of his entourage whiz on by. It
looked like they then plunged to earth way beyond the horizon.
The heat and winds are growing unbearable, but Atlas
stands his ground and carefully studies the events. Eliphaz
begs him and his son to come into the cave where the rest
of Atlas's entourage had taken shelter.

Eliphaz
Please, great King, come into the shelter!

Atlas
You go.

Eliphaz
I will stay with my King.

39

Atlas

No. You have the knowledge of
the people - the knowledge of the ages.
You must preserve our knowledge ...

Atlas looks around and sees the winds sweeping great
fires across his lands. He sees his great city of Poseidon
down on the plain being destroyed.

Atlas

... even if we cannot save our lands.
Go! And take my son.

Job

I'll stay with you.

Atlas

Go! Both of you!

Eliphaz hesitantly heads towards the cave. Job stays.

Atlas

Go!

Job starts to follow Eliphaz. As they reach the safety of
the cave, Job looks back at his father.
Suddenly the wind sweeps a gust of burning debris
onto Atlas and Atlas bursts into a great blaze of fire.
Job runs towards his father.
Too late.
Job stares in horror as the flames consume his father.
Then a smaller gust of burning dust strikes Job and
burns through his clothes, and into his skin.
Job staggers towards the cave and Eliphaz hurries over
to him and drags him into the cave.
And the great fire sweeps the entire area.

Great sheets of lighting flash and dance within the debris-laden atmosphere. Even greater bolts and sheets zap between earth and Satan and Satan's attendants.

The earth begins to shake. Parts of the mountain come tumbling down.

The mouth of the cave is sealed.

Figure 20: Job and his companions are sealed in the cave.

Figure 21: Ta-Wats watches in awe as the great balls of fire approach.

Western North America: May 5, 9619 BC

But some could not understand God's warning - and did not prepare.

As Satan approached near earth, the earth's atmosphere began to be drawn towards Satan - causing great hurricane-like winds.

Ta-Wats stood in the raging wind and watched as the approaching "shooting stars" got bigger and bigger. He will never forget the sight.

It must be some sort of a god.

It had a very long tail. It was surrounded by its helpers. They all twisted and undulated like the great serpents that they were!

They all glowed red hot.

They all spit fire at the earth. Grasses, trees - everything in sight began to burn.

Ta-Wats became very hot. The heat and great wind were sucking all the moisture from his body.

But he was too mesmerized to run. He stood against the heat and wind - and watched.

He watched as the serpents entered the earth's atmosphere and began to glow even brighter than the sun. Now he knew they were coming to get him. God must have sent them.

He knew that God would get him; make him pay for violating God's many rules. His violations flashed through his mind. He wondered which had finally been enough for God. Probably his taking young Ukria's squaw - in the woods that day.

The very large balls of fire, with their long flaming tails began to break up from the force and heat of the atmosphere. They broke up into even more "heads".

Ta-Wats knew he was guilty. He knew that his life was over. He dropped his traps and raised his open arms to God's fiery serpents.

Figure 22: Shock waves from the serpents roll Ta-Wats across the ground at a great speed..

The serpents seemed to speed up. They were now rushing towards him at almost blinding speeds. Their bright, fiery glow was beginning to blind him. He closed his eyes.

No help.

The bright glow penetrated his eyelids. He turned his head.

The serpents whizzed over his head and continued on their northwest to southeast path.

He opened his eyes and again looked at them.

Suddenly a noise louder than can be explained began to fill his ears, his head, his whole body - and an invisible supersonic shock wave knocked him to the ground.

The force from the wave rolled him at a very great speed across the ground. The vegetation and flying debris stirred up by the shock wave frayed his face and exposed skin. Blood began to seep from the wounds.

Finally he managed to hold on to a small tree and the wave passed on over him. He watched as the invisible wave raced across his land, continuing to stir up debris and to level trees.

Blood began to flow from the seepage wounds in his face and hands.

He looked again at God's serpents and watched them disappear beyond his horizon.

He finally managed to stand up against the raging wind and flying debris.

God had spared him.

He would retell this story many times - and it would eventually become the basis for the legends of many tribes of the Northwestern American Indians that we read about today, as presented in Chapters Four, Five and Seven.

Eastern North America: May 5, 9619 BC

Satan and his entourage continue over the North American continent. Many from the swarm of bodies accompanying Satan continue to break up at an ever increasing rate at they dip deeper into the earth's atmosphere. All glow with intense heat. One very large body explodes into millions of pieces.

Many Indians from many tribes watch as the "great serpent" and its attendants streak across their sky. And all hear its great cry; and many felt its invisible shock waves. And many watch the waves - now 2 (leading edge and trailing edge shock waves) for each "head" that it had broken into, as they streak across the lands.

Their descriptions of what thy saw were handed down as oral tribal legends.

Several thousand such legends have been documented. They reflect the various aspects of the heavenly bodies as seen by the many people, and at the different phases of their break up and impacts. They watch pieces hit the east coast of the North American continent; centered on the east coast of what is now South Carolina.

About 1,000,000 pieces hit the land there, making oval shaped craters along their northwest to southeast line of travel. Almost 500,000 of these "Carolina Bays", as depicted in Chapter Five are still very visible today.

Another 1,000,000 pieces are estimated to have landed in the Atlantic Ocean just off the coast of South Carolina. The 2 biggest pieces left very deep holes in the ocean floor that are still very visible today.

Figure 23: The Vela Supernova Remnant is today's view of Satan's original home in heaven!

Chapter 4
Why The War in Heaven

"Philosophers and theologians have yet to learn that a physical fact is as sacred as a moral principle."

J. Louis Agassiz

Did these events really happen? Was Satan really thrown out of heaven? Is there any scientific evidence?
Yes, yes, and yes.

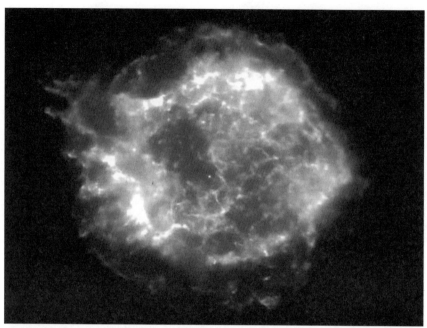

Figure 24: Cassiopeia was the last supernova is our galaxy.

Figure 25: The Crab Nebula is the remnant of a supernova that occurred in 1054 AD.

The Vela Supernova

A rather large, but otherwise common star in the constellation of Vela, situated about 45 light years away from our solar system, became a supernova and exploded sometimes between 14,300 and 11,000 years ago. This can be approximated by observable debris fields. The most likely date is 14,300 years ago.

The most visible remains of the supernova is the Vela Supernova Remnant as depicted (Figure 23). It is indeed interesting that it actually has the uncanny appearance of the popular conception of Satan!

(This view of Satan can be better seen in the color photographs, which can be obtained from UnKnownTruths.com as described in the back of this book.)

Supernovae occur at the end of the lives of massive stars, when they have exhausted their nuclear fuel. The star begins to collapse into its self and then explodes, releasing as much energy in a few days as is normally emitted in the same time period by the entire galaxy of billions of stars.

The typical remains are the nebulae as depicted. There is usually a pulsar imbedded near the nebula's center. Vela's pulsar is a rapidly spinning neutron star of intense density, but having a very small diameter. It spins about 11 times a second.

Such a supernova is not a rare event in the universe. Several have been observed in a single year. However supernovae are rare in our own Milky Way Galaxy. The last supernova in our galaxy was Cassiopeia, which was first viewable from earth in 1680 AD. It is 9 to 11 thousand light years from earth, near the edge of our Milky Way Galaxy, so it actually exploded sometime between 9323 and 11323 years ago.

51

Figure 26: The Hubble Space Telescope photographed
Supernova 1987A February 23, 1987.

Figure 27: Betelgeuse in The constellation Orion, is expected to be the next supernova in our galaxy.

In ancient Ethiopia, Cassiopeia (Figure 24) was believed to be the mother of Andromeda. We now recognize Andromeda as another galaxy and Cassiopeia as the remains of the youngest supernova in our Milky Way Galaxy.

An earlier supernova, first seen in 1054 AD, created the better-known Crab Nebula as depicted. It is about 6 thousand light years from earth; therefore it exploded almost 7 thousand years ago. Its pulsar spins about 30 times per second.

The Hubble Space Telescope photographed a more recent supernova, named "Super Nova 1987 A" for the year in which it became visible on earth. It is 167 thousand light years from earth, thus it exploded about 167 thousand years ago, with its light finally reaching earth February 23, 1987.

Betelgeuse is expected to be the next major star in our galaxy to become a supernova. It is 425 light years away. When it goes, it will be visible all day, and cast a shadow at night.

Betelgeuse makes up the right shoulder of the constellation Orion. It is interesting to note that Orion was a major feature in the religions of many ancient peoples, and is believed by many to be a model for the layout of the pyramids of Gaza in Egypt.

Figure 28: Some of the materials from the supernova were mutually attracted to each other by their gravities.

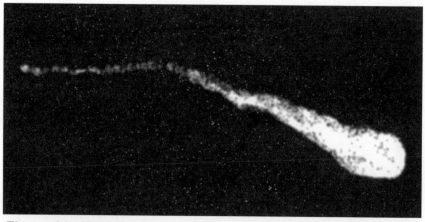

Figure 29: Eventually the near-by materials were pulled into the center of gravity of the mass and formed a collected stream of materials that appeared as a big-headed serpent with a long tail.

The Vela supernova probably ejected a mass of material about 1.4 times the size of our sun. Chunks of this material, calculated collectively to be a little larger than our earth, was hurled towards our solar system at an average speed of between 1/10 to 1/100 the speed of light. Calculations suggest that the most likely average speed was 1/62 the speed of light.

This mass of material would have been globs of glowing hot matter.

It would have been pulled into an elongated sphere by its own gravity, combined with the slightly varying velocities of adjacent materials.

Some of the adjacent materials, slightly farther away, would have then been attracted to this very large mass. These additional materials would have become a stream of trailing materials. After a time, this combined "chunk" of materials would have begun to appear to be the glowing hot, bigheaded serpent described in the ancient literature.

The heavens are full of supernova remnants. But none of them can match the interest of Vela! Vela was the ancient source of Satan, and now appears as the face of Satan!

Figure 30: The Vela Supernova spawned Satan.

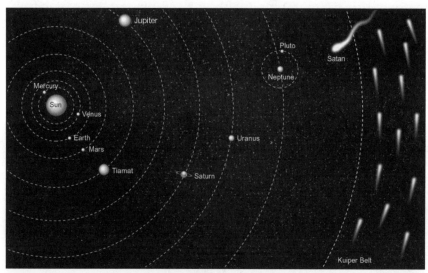

Figure 31: Satan's approach to the solar system was counter to the normal rotation of the planets and Kuiper Belt objects.

Kuiper Belt Encounters

This chunk, with its streaming tail of materials arrived in our solar system about 11,500 years ago. It is important to note that it was "going the wrong way", i.e. it was going in the opposite direction of the planets that orbit the sun. And it was going in an opposing direction to the sub-planets and other objects in the Kuiper Belt of objects out beyond the orbit of Pluto.

It is most likely that it encountered one or more bodies in the Kuiper Belt.

It is believed that there are millions of objects in this belt. Over 600 such objects have been spotted. Most of the objects are too small to be seen from earth, but it is estimated that 70,000 or more are at least 60 miles in diameter, and many are known to be 150 miles or more in diameter. One, dubbed KBO, with a diameter of 800 miles, was recently spotted.

Collisions with objects in the Kuiper Belt most likely fractured the main - and extended - body of the chunk, creating an even longer "tail" of materials. Some of these smaller pieces would have had a tendency to orbit, in a corkscrew like fashion, about the larger mass. These smaller pieces would also further disperse over time and form an ever increasingly longer tail. Such a swarm of objects would become to look more and more like a big-headed (eventually multi-headed) serpent with a long undulating tail.

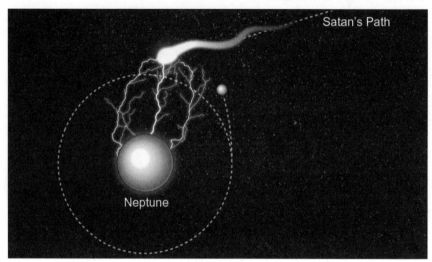

Figure 32: Neptune and Satan exchanged great discharges.

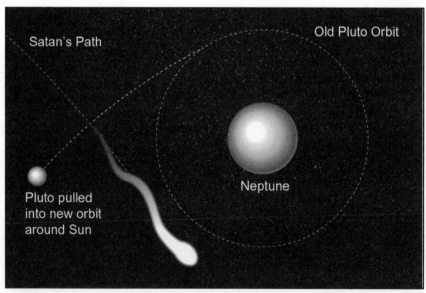

Figure 33: Satan pulled Pluto from its orbit around Neptune and set it on its own destiny (orbit).

Neptune Encounter

At the time that the chunk entered our solar system, the outermost planet was Neptune. It is believed that Pluto, currently the ninth, and farthest out planet, was then a moon of Neptune. It has also been speculated that Neptune had earlier captured Pluto from the Kuiper Belt.

As the chunk continued on its path towards the sun, the gravity from the giant Neptune began to influence it. Neptune is 17.14 times more massive than is earth.

When it was close enough to Neptune, the two bodies began to exchange great lighting-like electromagnetic discharges, as the bodies tended to equalize their very different charges.

The gravity of the chunk exerted a pull on Neptune's moon Pluto and caused Pluto to be pulled from its orbit around Neptune, and slung into its own orbit around the sun.

Pluto has the most irregular orbit of all the planets. It is the only planet that crosses the orbit of another planet, in that it regularly still crosses Neptune's orbit, as it did when it originally rotated around Neptune as its moon.

The plane of Pluto's orbit also deviates most from the planes of the other planets. It is 17.148 degrees from earth's orbit plane.

So there is considerable evidence that Pluto was a moon of Neptune that was slung into its own - irregular - orbit by a large body passing close-by. The irregular orbits of Neptune's remaining two moons, Triton and Nereid, also support such a disturbance as would be caused by this passing.

Neptune's mass, more than 13 times the mass of the chunk, plus its very close proximity at the passing, presented a gravitational field that caused Neptune's tides of gravity to break-up the chunk into even more of a swarm of many pieces of greatly varying sizes.

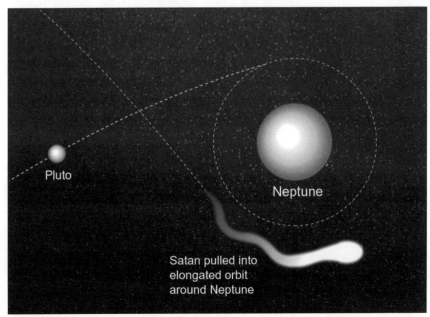

Figure 34: Neptune's great gravity caused Satan to begin to orbit about Neptune in an elongated ellipse.

Neptune's gravity at this close approach was very much greater than the distant sun. This resulted in the chunk's path being altered towards a tendency to orbit Neptune on a highly elliptical orbit.

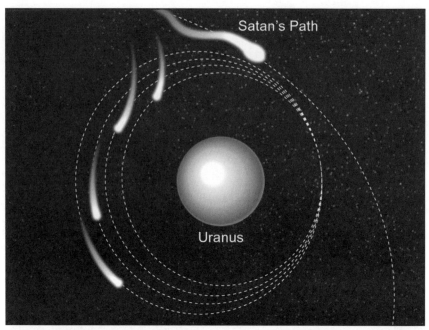

Figure 35: Uranus pulls four "moons" from Satan.

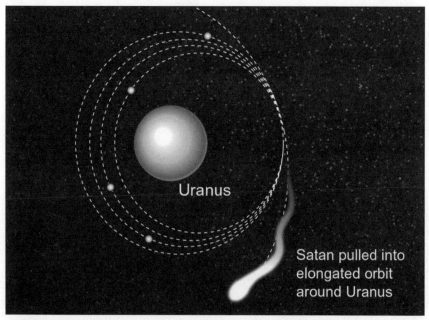

Figure 36: Uranus pulls Satan into a new orbit.

Uranus Encounter

The chunk, on this altered orbit, approached the orbit of Uranus.

Uranus has about 85 percent of the mass, and thus gravitational pull of Neptune; but when the chunk came near Uranus, its attraction was much greater than the more distant Neptune or the distant sun.

Uranus was already passing the possible impact point, but the bodies passed close enough to exchange electro-magnetic discharges and Uranus's gravitational pull was sufficient to detach at least 4 pieces from the broken chunk.

This encounter:

1. Provided Uranus with at least 4 of its 17 moons;
2. Turned Uranus's axis of rotation to 97 degrees 55 minutes (compared to earth's 23 degrees 27 minutes);
3. Distorted Uranus's magnetic field 59 degrees from its axis of rotation, and 15 percent away from the planet's center (It had also produced a similar off-center field in Neptune.)
4. Again altered the chunk's orbit to an elongated ellipse, now about Uranus.

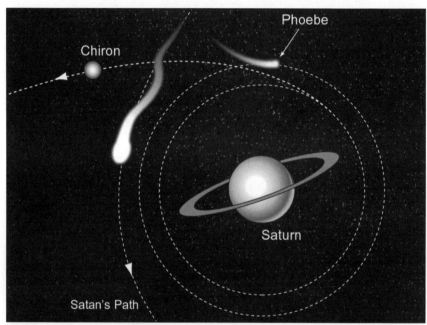

Figure 37: Chiron is pulled from Saturn and placed in its own destiny (orbit) about the sun. Saturn pulls a piece from Satan for its moon, Phoebe.

Saturn Encounter

Saturn's mass is over 6.5 times that of Uranus; so soon after the chunk left the vicinity of Uranus, the primary gravitational attraction came from Saturn.

Saturn's great mass - 80 times greater than the chunk's - altered the chunk's path, causing a very near pass-by. One of Saturn's moons, Chiron, which was in its orbit far from Saturn, passed extremely close to the chunk, and was pulled out of orbit and sent on its own destiny (orbit) - around the sun - similar to the manner in which the chunk had torn Pluto from Neptune and placed it in its own orbit.

Chiron was known in ancient times as Kronus's (Saturn's) son. (How did they know that tiny Chiron had been Saturn's moon?)

When Chiron was later "rediscovered" by modern science, it was deemed too small to be called a planet. (Many are questioning whether Pluto should be called a planet. It is only 1,419 miles in diameter.)

As the chunk continued to approach Saturn, gravitational tides began to fracture the chunk and parts of it began to disperse. Saturn's great gravity then pulled a piece of the broken up chunk into orbit around it.

It is interesting that this new moon of Saturn's, Phoebe, orbits in a retrograde orbit; i.e. circles in the opposite direction of the other moons.

It is also possible, that this piece of the chunk, i.e. Phoebe, may have been one of the pieces that had been orbiting the chunk when the chunk approached Saturn. It may have been captured in one of the chunk's previous encounters.

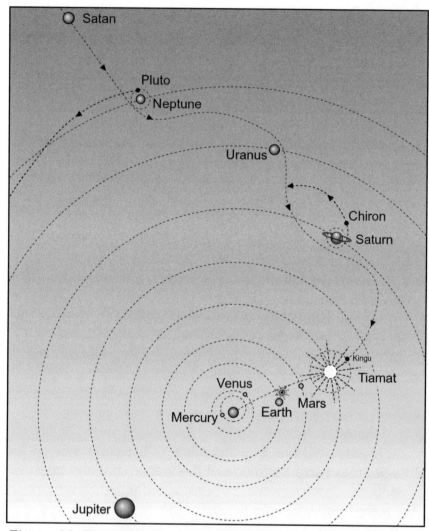

Figure 38: The planets continuously changed Satan's orbit.

Wrong Way Orbit

The chunk then continued on its elongated orbit about Saturn until it was far enough away from Saturn that the gravitational fields of Tiamat and the Sun became more dominate, and began to pull the chunk's orbit back towards Tiamat.

(At this time, the giant planet Jupiter was in its orbit on the other side of the sun.)

So the chuck's orbital path had by this time experienced the following transitions:

1. Hurled from the supernova generally towards the solar system;
2. Drawn towards the sun;
3. Drawn towards Neptune and established in an elliptical orbit about Neptune - but before it could complete even half an orbit;
4. Drawn towards Uranus and established in an elongated ellipse about Uranus - but again, before it could complete much of the orbit;
5. Drawn towards the very much larger Saturn, and again, before it could complete much of the orbit;
6. Drawn towards Tiamat as Tiamat's pull became stronger as the chunk left the vicinity of Saturn.

All of this time, the chunk's orbit was "going the wrong way", relative to all the planets. There are several ancient accounts that refer to this wrong way orbit, including the writings of Ovid (see later).

Figure 39: The Tiamat impact was very visible from earth.

Tiamat: The Destroyed Planet

At the time of the chunk's intrusion into the solar system, there was a large planet in the orbit now occupied by the asteroid belt. The ancients knew about it and had named it Tiamat. It had a mass 90 times that of the chunk, so it soon became the most dominate attracting force.

Modern science does not know about Tiamat because this planet was destroyed, as described below, before the modern era.

But very compelling evidence shows that Tiamat was well known to the ancient world. It was the brightest star in the heavens (after the sun and moon). It was believed to be the mother god, and was widely worshipped in the ancient world.

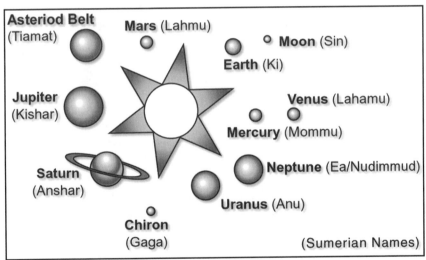

Figure 40: The chart of planets from ancient Sumer clearly shows that they knew of Tiamat.

69

The combined pulls from Tiamat and the sun turned the chunk from its orbit about Saturn and the sun, and caused it to approach Tiamat as depicted in Figure 38. The two bodies exchanged great electromagnetic discharges to equalize their very different electromagnetic charges.

The great mass of Tiamat forced an impact. Debris was hurled all over the where. Some stayed in orbit around the sun and became the asteroid belt. Some experienced various elongated orbits about the sun and added to the number of comets and other materials that orbit and "wander" about the solar system. Some escaped from the solar system.

But most of the debris from the collision had too little velocity to remain in orbit - because the angle of impact had countered each body's velocity. This resulting mass from the two bodies began to spiral towards the sun.

One large member of this mass was Tiamat's principle moon, Kingu. As the remains of Tiamat and the chunk spiraled towards the sun, Kingu continued to orbit - in a corkscrew fashion - the combined mass of Tiamat and the chunk.

From earth, the sky appeared to be filled with heavenly bodies, i.e. pieces from the collision. There were probably many, many thousands; perhaps millions. However, many were too small to be seen from earth, and many were clumped close enough together such that they would appear as one. All together, the stream of materials appeared as a great undulating, fiery serpent.

Kingu and other objects orbiting the materials from the collision made the "serpent's" motion appear very dynamic.

As this now extended stream of undulating materials spiraled towards the sun, it approached the orbit of Mars.

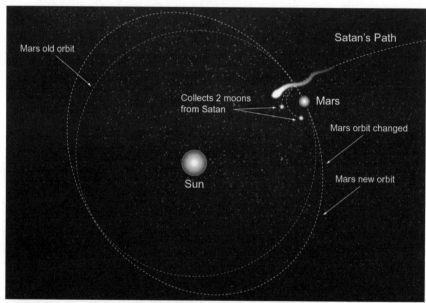

Figure 41: Satan sends Mars into a more eccentric orbit. Mars gets two moons from the chunk.

Mars Encounter

At this time Mars was too far from its orbit crossing point to cause an impact, but the bodies passed close enough to exchange electromagnetic discharges. The passing was also close enough to:

1. Greatly reduce Mars' magnetic field;
2. Fracture Mars' crust;
3. Upset Mars' rotational equilibrium such that it was slowed from its then 8 hour day to slightly more than a 24 hour day;
4. Send Mars into a much more eccentric orbit;
5. Cause Mars to pull 2 very irregularly shaped, jagged, pieces of rock from the stream of Tiamat and chunk debris.

These 2 moons of Mars are the most jagged moons in the known universe.

Figure 42: Satan's closest approach filled the sky from horizon to horizon.

Figure 43: The multi-headed serpent view probably gave rise to the hydra.

Earth Encounter

The stream of material, still being orbited by Tiamat's moon, Kingu, continued on its path towards the sun, and earth.

It was clearly visible, not only in the night sky, but had become visible in full daylight. Ancient literature state that Kingu and other "orbiting objects" made the chunk's shape continuously change.

> *"For 10 nights it looked like a man.*
>
> *For 10 nights it looked like a golden horned bull.*
>
> *For 10 nights it looked like a white horse with golden ears."*

Figure 44: Ancients recorded their view of Satan(Marduk).

It would be hard to believe that this "intruder" is not the origin of the serpent and dragon myths, legends, and stories.

Stories of the various views were handed down through the ages - and distorted - re-imagined. This resulted in the many stories of serpents, dragons, hydra and the famous paintings of the "War in Heaven" and "Satan thrown from Heaven".

It was indeed a frightening, awe inspiring experience.

The combined mass of the remaining parts of Tiamat and the chunk would have been much larger than the earth.

This mass was at least 350 times larger than our moon, and probably 4 times as close, making it appear to be 1400 times the size of the moon!

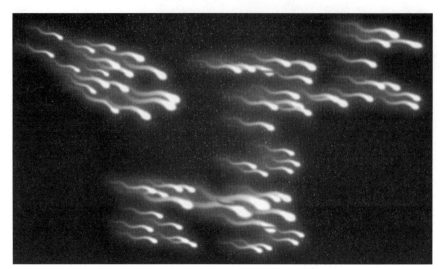

Figure 45: The probable views from various approach distances seen by various people on various parts of earth.

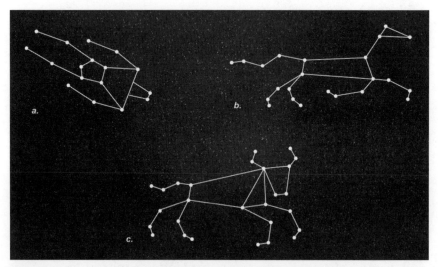

Figure 46: The 'interpretations" from the viewer's imaginations.

And because of the energy from the supernova, its several impacts, and its very close approach, it appeared to be glowing brighter than the sun!

Since the earth did not totally disintegrate, it has been calculated that the great mass passed no closer than about 60,000 miles from earth.

Even at a distance of 60,000 miles, its closest approach view would have spanned from horizon to horizon!

Figure 47: Satan and his entourage create chaos on earth.

Chapter 5
Chaos on Earth

"They fought from heaven; the stars in their courses fought against Sisera (our intelect)."
Judges 5:20

Satan created the greatest chaos that mankind has ever experienced. Most of our knowledge was destroyed.

The First Winds

As Satan approached earth, earth's atmosphere began to be pulled by gravity towards the large stream of the spiraling material. These materials were more than 50 times the size of the earth.

The winds continuously increased until they reached super-hurricane force.

The winds were initially strongest over the North American Continent because of Satan's approach, i.e. from northwest to southeast, first nearing earth on the northwest corner of the North American Continent. But all of earth experienced strong winds. These winds caused damages much greater than the damage we experience from our strongest hurricanes and tornados of today.

They eventually built up to intensities strong enough to sweep most surface materials into violent debris clouds and redeposit some of them hundreds of miles from their original positions. These new deposits also contained materials from the chunk and from Tiamat.

Trees were pulled up by the roots and strewn many miles away. Entire forests were swept away.

The winds eroded away sand and earthen hills down to base rock. Sand and grit in the winds polished rocks, and in some cases eroded them away completely.

Even large boulders were blown miles from their normal positions.

The Mayans named these severe winds after their god Hurakan. A corruption of this name became hurricane.

The Mesopotamians said that their god:

"Marduk created the evil wind, and tempest, and the hurricane, and the fourfold wind, and the sevenfold wind, and the whirlwind, and the wind which has no equal."

80

The violent winds made extremely loud noises. North American Indians remember a monster with a whistle in his mouth.

The Electromagnetic Discharges

Enormous electromagnetic discharges flashed between earth and the various components of the swarm of materials from Tiamat and the chunk. These discharges became ever more violent as the materials approached nearer to earth. The severe lighting and unbelievable noise sent many scurrying to caves, rocks, and other possible shelters. This may have been the major warning that most people received, and may have resulted in more people being saved than did any other factor.

These ever-increasing discharges created great heat.

Heat and Evaporation

The lakes and rivers began to evaporate. The seas steamed. This added to the imbalance in electromagnetic charge, and caused the discharges to continue, creating even more heat.

The heat became enormous. All shallow rivers and lakes evaporated completely. The seas and oceans continued to steam and parts of them boiled away.

The earth's surface was heated to such a degree that water within rocks exploded the rocks, adding to the swirling debris.

Fires and Debris

Grasses, trees, and other combustibles burst into flame, starting many great fires. This added to the velocity of the great winds, creating super-hurricane firestorm intensities on various parts of earth.

The great winds swept up great qualities of dust, vegetation, dirt, and even large rocks, and carried them in scouring debris over much of the earth. Debris of various types filled valleys and depressions and piled drifts across the countryside.

The combustible materials, blowing in the great hurricanes, fed the fires, causing them to burn much of everything encountered.

Crust Fractures and Earthquakes

The gravitational tidal waves within the earth caused by the close approach of Tiamat and the chunk, resulted in great fractures in the earth's crust. The great tectonic plates broke into more pieces.

Earthquakes occurred all over the where!

Thousands of volcanoes erupted, spewing rocks, dust, smoke, and lava into the building chaos. These materials began to rain down on the surface in depths of thousands of feet in some places.

Great avalanches of sand, dirt, and rock raced across the land at over 200 miles per hour. Tsunamis raced across the seas at over 500 miles per hour.

Escaping gases ignited, adding to the great fires.

Boiling hot steam, filled with grit, sprayed about the areas, "polishing" stones and destroying most materials in their paths.

Boiling mud and mudslides flowed into many depressions.

Lava and magma flowed liberally.

The earth's poles flipped and reversed the magnetic charges, creating even more heat. The firestorms were intensified. Now all of the seas began to boil, further evaporating.

The cracks in the earth's crust became more numerous, and larger. The tectonic plates fractured more and moved independently of each other, thrusting up great mountains and sinking great landmasses.

Areas in the Himalayan Mountains and in the Alps were thrust up an additional 6,000 feet. Mountains in China (Bayuan Kara Shan) thrust up an additional 6,500 feet. The Sierra Nevada and Cascades in California and Oregon also gained heights of an additional 6,500 feet. The Tibetan Plateau increased elevations by 9,750 feet. Alpine peaks increased by 13,000 feet, as did the Andes.

The Rockies were thrust eastward by 8 miles.

And great areas sank, replacing the material that had been thrust up in the increased elevations. Extremely large landmasses in the Pacific Ocean sank. The floor of the North Atlantic Ocean sank over 9,000 feet. The land about the Azores sank almost 3 miles.

Great fords were opened in the Scandinavian areas. The Gobi Desert changed from a lake to a dry plain that later became a desert. Some of the great ancient rivers of India disappeared.

Almost the entire surface of the earth was changed.

The atmosphere became saturated with smoke, dust, water vapor, and debris. This further intensified the discharges between earth, earth's atmosphere, and the various bodies still approaching earth.

And the heat was even further intensified. Most of the small seas evaporated completely, and much of the oceans boiled away.

The heat was far too great for any of the water vapor to condense to form rain.

Some of the cracks in the earth's crust opened further, swallowing everything nearby. Some shifted; then closed on their swallowed materials. Some stayed open and became the great fords and locks we still have today.

Many of the volcanic eruptions and earthquakes could be felt 1000 miles away. All of the earth trembled with shocks and reverberating aftershocks.

And some of the seismic activity started then is still going on today.

Figure 48: The waters of the oceans pile up towards Satan.

Great Ocean Waves Form

The great mass of Tiamat and the chunk continued towards earth. Water remaining in the oceans was drawn into a pile towards the great approaching masses to form a water thickness many miles high. It tended to follow the stream of materials as the materials passed close to earth's surface. But the water could not move fast enough to follow. It continued to pile up until the stream of masses passed.

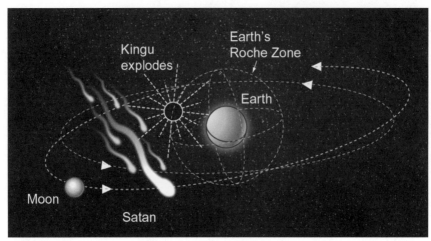

Figure 49: Kingu enters the Earth's Roche Zone and explodes

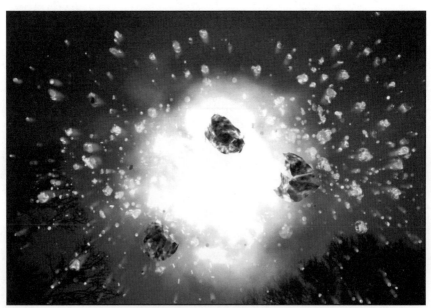

Figure 50: Kingu splits into several major heads and millions of smaller pieces.

Impacts

The most likely path of the mass of materials can be determined by careful studies of still existing impact craters and debris deposits. Satan's path was from the north-west to the south-east.

As Satan passed overhead at an altitude of about 60,000 miles, Kingu continued to orbit the primary mass.

The spirally orbiting Kingu came within earth's Roche Zone, i.e. within 8 to 12 thousands miles of earth. The gravitational tidal waves caused Kingu to explode. It broke into three or more major chunks and millions of smaller pieces. At least two of the large pieces and at least a million of the smaller pieces fell to earth.

Two very large pieces of Kingu fell into the ocean east of the Carolinas and formed the large craters still visible in the Atlantic Ocean.

Some pieces continued on with the great mass of Tiamat and the chunk. Some scattered and became meteors and asteroids.

Many pieces of Tiamat and the chunk were also drawn to, and impacted the earth.

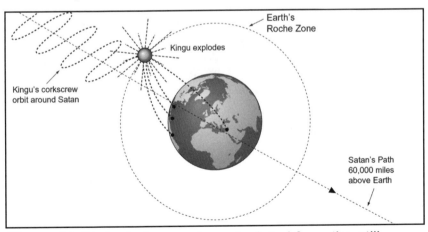

Figure 51: Trajectories can be calculated from the still existing impact craters.

Perhaps the most visible remaining impact craters are the so-called Carolina Bays and similar craters.

Such impact craters are not that uncommon. A great crater in the Gulf of Mexico, just off the Yucatan Peninsular marks the impact credited with the destruction of the dinosaurs.

The most visible crater is the result of an impact about 50,000 years ago in Arizona.

Smaller objects enter Earth's atmosphere daily, but are usually burned up as they enter the earth's atmosphere. It is estimated that over 10,000 tons of impact material enter earth's atmosphere every year.

During the subject great disaster, of course, the raining debris was enormous. In addition to the great chunks from Kingu and parts of Marduk and Tiamat, there were millions of smaller gravel-like stones, mud and waters that fell on much of the earth.

All of this activity added even more heat.

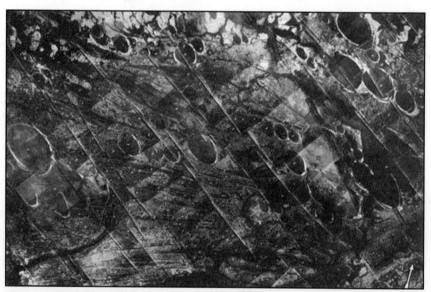

Figure 52: The impacts of Kingu in the "Carolina Bays" are still very visible.

90

Earth's moon is drawn towards the mass and pulled into a wider orbit.

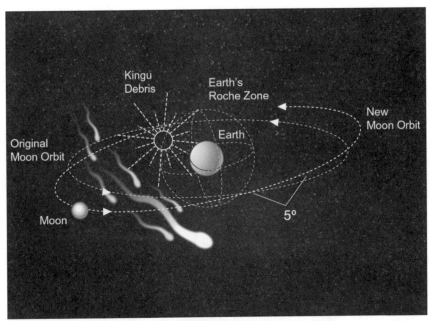

Figure 53: Satan pulls earth's moon into a wider orbit.

Figure 54: This crater in Arizona is one of many impacts experienced by earth.

Figure 55: Great waves raced across all but the highest mountains.

Great Waves Wash Over The Land

The rest of the great masses whizzed on past earth, headed towards a collision with the sun.

When the stream of materials had passed, the pile of waters of the oceans collapsed and sent great waves, some over 3 miles high initially, over all landmasses except for the highest mountains. Great whales and other sea animals were washed hundreds of feet above sea level and deposited in cracks and depressions far inland.

The great waves continued to sweep across the face of the earth until they finally, after several cycles, wore themselves down to "ripples" that remained contained within the ocean basins.

The waves extinguished most of the fires, but the heat was still far too great for the evaporated water to condense and fall as rain.

Darkness

Thousands of volcanoes continued to pour smoke and debris into the water vapor loaded atmosphere. The resulting debris cloud totally blocked out the sun and all heavenly bodies.

It stayed too hot for most of the water to evaporate.

The blackness lasted for years.

The Central American Aztecs remember that:

"After the destruction of the fourth sun, the world plunged into darkness during the space of twenty-five years."

Analyzing data from volcanoes over the last few hundred years, suggests that total blackness probably lasted for at least 3 years - as stated in ancient Russian literature. When some light did return, the American Indian legends state that:

... the light was quite as scanty as it had been down
below (in the caves where they had escaped the disaster),
for there was as yet no heaven, no sun, nor moon, nor stars.

It is likely that it took several decades before the sun light returned to near the conditions of today.

Gradual Cooling

Gradually the enormous heat dissipated as it radiated from the tops of the debris clouds at a greater rate than heat could be absorbed from the blocked sun.

The water vapor condensed about the debris and it finally began to rain.

It wasn't too long before the rains had increased to extremely hard downpours.

And the great flood of legend really happen.

The Flood

It has been calculated that more than half of all waters on earth had evaporated and formed "the canopy" of clouds that blacked out the sun. It is likely that additional waters were also brought to earth by "debris" from Tiamat.

When it finally began to cool enough for the water vapor to condense, the clouds would have been very heavy all the way down to the ground; giving rise to the "collapsed sky" stories found in most of the descriptions of the time.

It is easy to believe that it then rained for "forty days and forty nights" as stated in the Bible.

This very heavy downpour that lasted for a very long period, which followed the great waves that washed across the land, is the firm foundation for the many legends of the worldwide flood.

The Bitter Cold

The imbalance in heat radiated, versus heat absorbed, increased exponentially such that it reached the point where it almost suddenly got very cold.

As the rate of cooling became faster, the rain turned to sleet, hail, and snow. Everything became blackened from the great masses of debris in the clouds.

Most of the earth became bitter cold. And it remained bitter cold - and very dark - for years.

Return of The Sun

Finally most of the water vapor in the clouds condensed and fell as snow - and some of the debris was washed from the clouds.

The sun begins to show through the still debris-laden clouds.

Gradually it begins to get warmer. The snows and ice begin to melt and cause additional floods. These secondary flooding conditions continued for over a year.

And it was decades before the skies were generally clear of all the debris from the disaster and from the volcanoes that continued to erupt.

Earth's climate has not yet - after 11,500 years - returned to the pre-disaster norm of the Golden Age.

The disaster destroyed almost all life, of all kinds. The face and internal structure of the earth was changed forever.

But some humans did survive, and they recorded their memories.

Figure 56: Eventually the sun comes shinning through.

Figure 57: There was a War in Heaven.

Chapter 6
Ancient Documentation of The War in Heaven

"The trouble with the world is not that people know too little, but that they know so many things that ain't so."
Mark Twain

Many elements of this great disaster have been recorded in the literature of man. A major problem, of course, is that the literature has been copied - and edited, perhaps unconsciously, down through the ages. Later scribes and copiers, who did not witness the events, have created significant alterations. We must keep this in mind as we review the ancient documents.

Figure 58: Ancient clay tablets from Babylon and Sumer tell the story of the disaster.

Sumerian Enuma Elish: Marduk

One of the oldest written records of the disaster was found in an ancient library in Nineveh. When archeologists excavated this library of King Assurbanipal, they found the first tablets dating back to about 650 BC, but it was acknowledged in the tablets that they had been copied from a much older text. Later excavations in ancient Sumer found incomplete clay tablet fragments that told essentially the same story. Piecing them together, they were able to translate The Enuma Elish of ancient Sumer.

The Enuma Elish consists of seven clay tablets plus various fragments. It is a very repetitive document. This repetitiveness and some additional lines have been omitted for the sake of brevity, but otherwise the translations given here are word for word.

The Enuma Elish has erroneously been referred to as "The Epic of Creation", but as noted by translator L. W. King, the epic "took place after men had been created and cities had been built."

There have been several slightly varying translations. Here is presented the basic story, with word for word quotes from some of the translations.

The first tablet describes the gods fear that their mother, Tiamat, is plotting war against some of the other gods. It is believed that Tiamat was considered to be the mother of the gods because she was, at the time, the brightest star in the heavens - except for the sun and moon.

The other gods try to dissuade her, but to no avail. So they call upon a new god, Marduk.

"In the Chamber of Fates, the place of Destinies,
A god was engendered, most able and wisest of gods;
In the heart of the Deep was Marduk created."

101

Figure 59: Marduk is "glorified" with electromagnetic flashes.

That is, Marduk came from outer space in accordance with the description of the exploding star Vela described in Chapter Four. He could be seen from earth because he was glowing hot from Vela's supernova and from probable encounters with bodies in the Kuiper Belt as is also described in Chapter Four.

"Alluring was his figure,
Sparkling the lift of his eyes;
Lordly was his gait (orbit), commanding as of olden times ...
Greatly exalted was he above the gods,
exceeding throughout ...
His members were enormous, he was exceeding tall ...
When he moved his lips fire blazed forth."

A separate tablet fragment further describes his size:

"Fifty kaspu (about 350 miles) in his length,
One kaspu (about 6.5 miles) in his height,
Six cubits (about 9 feet) in his mouth,
Twelve cubits (about 18 feet) his ..."

Here the text is lost.
When he entered the solar system, the planets:

"... Heaped upon him their awesome flashes ...
(and he became) clothed with the halo of ten gods."

This is believed to describe the enormous exchanges of electromagnetic charges between Marduk and the planets - which caused Marduk to glow even brighter; ten times brighter than a normal god (planet).

Marduk continued into the solar system, passing Neptune and Uranus, which:

"Heaped upon him their awesome flashes ..."

Then he approached Saturn:

"And he drew nigh and stood before Ansar (Saturn).
Ansar beheld him and his heart was filled with joy,
He kissed him on the lips and his fear departed
from him."

And Saturn praises Marduk.

"O my son, who knoweth all wisdom,
... speedily set out upon thy way ..."

And Marduk takes this opportunity to ask:

"If I, your avenger,
Conquer Tiamat and save your lives,
Appoint an assembly to proclaim my destiny
supreme."

Ansar (Saturn) opened his mouth,
And unto Gaga (a moon of Saturn), his minister,
spake the word, "O Gaga, thou minister that
rejoices my spirits, unto Lahmu (Mars) and
Lahamu (Venus) will I send thee."

Saturn instructs Gaga to go tell the other gods - and:

"Make ready; for a feast, at a banquet let them
sit ..."

Saturn's moon Gaga (Chiron) is released from its orbit around Saturn, and injected into its own orbit around the sun - as described in Chapter Four.

And Marduk approaches Tiamat.

"Go, and cut off the life of Tiamat,
And let the wind carry her blood into secret
places."

That is, parts of her are to be scattered into unknown space.

And Marduk proceeded.

"He set the lighting in front of him,
With burning flame he filled his body.
He made a net to enclose the inward parts of
Tiamat, ..."

Marduk and Tiamat exchange electromagnetic charges. Their gravities act as nets to attract each other.

As Marduk gets closer, Tiamat's moon, Kingu, is pulled from its orbit and attracted to Marduk.

"The Lord (Marduk) drew nigh,
He gazed upon the inward parts of Tiamat,
He perceived the muttering of Kingu, her spouse.
As Marduk gazed, Kingu was troubled in his
gait (orbit),
His will was destroyed and his (regular)
motions ceased."

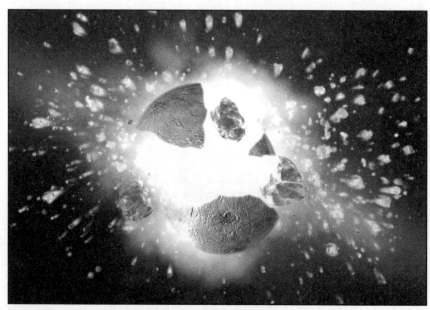

Figure 60: Tiamat is torn to pieces.

And Marduk says:

"Stand! I and thou, let us join in battle!"
"When Tiamat heard these words,
She was like one possessed,
She lost her reason."
"Tiamat uttered wild, piercing cries,
She trembled and shook to her very foundations."
"Tiamat and Marduk, the wisest of gods, advanced
against one another;
They pressed on to single combat, they
approached for battle."

This describes the extremely violent electromagnetic discharges between the two bodies as they got closer and closer. It produced great heat and thunderous acoustics that could even be heard on earth.

And the battle rages:

"The Lord (Marduk) spread out his net and caught
her;"
"The Evil Wind that was behind him he let loose in
her face."
"As she opened her mouth, Tiamat, to devour him -
He drove the Evil Wind so that she closed not her
lips.
The Fierce Storm Winds then filled her belly.
And her courage was taken from her,
And her mouth she opened wide.
He shot there through an arrow,
It tore her belly,
It cut through her insides,
Tore into her womb.
Having thus subdued her, her life breath he
extinguished."

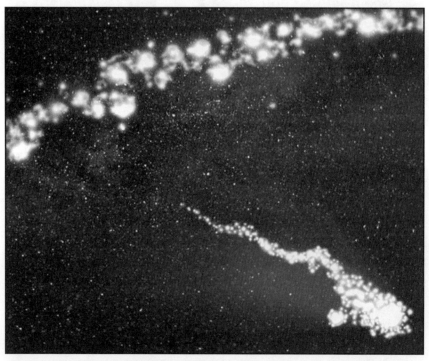

Figure 61: Marduk blasts Tiamat into millions of pieces to form the "hammered necklace".

The "Evil Wind", the "Fierce Storm Winds", and the "arrow" were parts of the trail of materials following the chunk as described in Chapter Four.

The gravitational tides caused the surface of Tiamat to crack, "open her mouth", and the various materials impacted with Tiamat.

Marduk tore Tiamat apart and:

"And caused the North Wind to bear it to places that have been unknown."

That is, outer space. And other pieces of her he:

"Locking them together, as watchmen he stationed them ...
He bent Tiamat's tail to form the Great Band as a bracelet."

The explosion of the impact, coupled with the even more violent electromagnet discharges and gravitational interactions, spread much of the materials into "the Great Band as a bracelet." That is, the asteroid belt, which now occupies the previous orbit of Tiamat.

But much of the resulting material followed Marduk:

"The gods, her helpers who marched at her side, ...
Found themselves ensnared ..."
"He took them captive, he broke their weapons;
In the net they were caught and in the snare they sat down ...
They were held in bondage."

They followed Marduk on his path towards the sun. And as for Tiamat's moon, Kingu:

"He took from him the Tablets of Destiny ...
He sealed them with a seal and in his own breast he
laid them."

That is, Marduk changed Kingu's orbit. The Tablets of Destiny have been determined to mean the fixed destiny of a fixed patrol, or orbit.

Kingu now followed Mardu and the remains of Tiamat in a corkscrew type orbit as described in Chapter Four.

> **This is the almost unbelievable written account of the destruction of the great planet, Tiamat!**

Figure 62: The ancients recorded the destruction of Tiamat!

Figure 63: Early statues show Marduk as a fierce non-human creature.

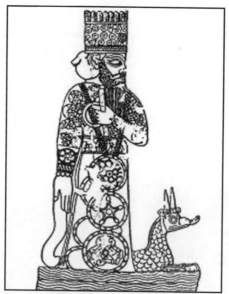

Figure 64: Later we see Marduk presented as a human-like god.

And so the planet Tiamat was removed from the heavens, never to be seen again.

And Marduk?

We know that Marduk, the celestial chunk, then disturbed and passed earth and went on to impact the sun - as described in Chapter Four.

But:

"He conquered Tiamat,
He troubled and ended her life,
In the future of mankind,
When the days grow old,
May this be heard without ceasing;
May it hold sway forever!"

And thus Marduk became the principal god of ancient Sumer.

Initially he was depicted as a fierce god, with the head of a serpent, the body of a reptile, the front legs of a lion and the back legs of an eagle. But through the ages, he became more human.

India's Rigveda: Indra

It is believed that the Rigveda of ancient India was copied from earlier documents. It tells of the battle between the great god Indra and the mighty serpent Vritra.

Vritra had stolen water from the earth. (Possibly the memory of the great evaporation period when Satan was approaching earth.) Indra rode forth to do battle with Vritra. After a long battle, Indra destroyed Vritra and slit him open. Great floods of water fell from the skies. Indra became the chief god of ancient India.

It is interesting to note that Indra's heaven was in the clouds above the sacred mountain Meru. This is the same mountain associated with Atlantis.

From the Rigveda we read that the gods realized that they could not hold their power until Vritra was destroyed. This is almost certainly an echo of the same message from the gods described in the Enuma Elish.

The gods had the artisan god, Twashtri prepare a weapon for Indra. Twashtri built the weapon and spoke to Indra:

"With this, the best of weapons, O exalted one, reduce that fierce foe of the gods to ashes! And, having slain the foe, rule thou happily the entire domain of heaven, O chief of the celestials, with those that follow thee."

Indra heads into battle and finds that Vritra is surrounded by Danavas (demons) that look like great mountain peaks. The battle ensues, with Indra first attacking the horde of Danavas. Indra drove them into the sea. Indra then kills Vritra.

I have slain Vritra, O ye hast'ning Maruts;
I have grown mighty through my own great vigour;
I am the hurler of the bolt of Thunder -
For man flow freely now the gleaming waters.

Then on earth his worshippers praised him:

I will extol the manly deeds of Indra;
The first was when the Thunder stone he wielded
And smote the Dragon; he released the waters,
He opened the channels of the breasted mountains.

He smote the Dragon Vritra in its fortress.
Twashtri had shaped for him the thunder weapon -
Then rushing freely like to bellowing castle,
The gladsome waters to the sea descended.

The smitten monster fell amidst the torrents,
That pause nor stay, forever surging onward;
Then Vritra covered by the joyful billows
Was carried to the darksome deeps of Ocean.

This does indeed sound like a simplified revision of the Enuma Elish, perhaps written several centeries later, and incorporating ancient India's principal god.

Norse Poetic Edda: The Serpent

The Norse Eddas are considered to be among the greatest of the world's literature. Most were written about 1000 years ago, but it is clear they were taken from very ancient literature. One of their great stories seems to parallel other stories of the great disaster.

For the sake of brevity, only excerpts are given here:

The war I remember, the first in the world,
When the gods with spears had smitten Gollveig,
And in the hall of Hor had burned her,
Three times burned, and three times born,
Oft and again, yet ever she lives.

Here Gollveig has been interpreted as "the one who refines gold by fire", and Hor "the High One".

Yggdrasil shakes, and shiver on high
The ancient limbs, and the giant is loose;
To the head of Mim does Othin give heed
But the kinsman of Surt shall slay him soon.

Yggdrasil is the axis of the earth. The head of Mim is the severed head of a water god that can talk and give advice to Othin. Othin is the chief of the gods. Surt is the giant who rules the fire-world.

Against the serpent goes Othin's son.

The sun turns black, earth sinks in the sea,
The hot stars down from heaven are whirled;
Fierce grows the steam and life-feeding flame,
Till fire leaps high about heaven itself.

This is a quite precise description of what happened in the disaster!

The poem then tells that the sun came back and everything became good again.

Norse Elder Edda: Fenris-Wolf and Midgard-Serpent

Another version in the Eddas tells:

Then it shall come to pass that the earth will shake so violently
That the trees will be torn up by the roots,
The mountains will topple down,
And all bonds and fetters will be broken and snapped.
The Fenris-wolf (one of the fragments) gets loose.
The sea rushes over the earth,
For the Midgard-serpent (another fragment) writhes in giant rage,
And seeks to gain the land.

It would be hard to believe that these are not describing the great disaster - rewritten many centuries later in terms of the gods of the ancient Norse.

Persia's Tistrya

Avestic scriptures of ancient Persia tell of the Evil One, Angra Mainyu that created a mighty serpent, Tistrya, that assaulted and deranged the sky and sent snow and vehement destroying frost. The gods warned Yima that this was going to happen.

Tistrya was called:

"The leader of the stars against the planets."

Egypt's Osiris

Egypt has a similar story of a fight between Osiris, the sun god, and Set, the evil one. Set wins and cuts Osiris's body into 14 parts and scatters them about the earth. Osiris's consort, wife and sister, finds the parts and helps resurrect Osiris in the form of his son Horus.

The basic belief is that ancient Egypt worshipped the sun god Osiris. When the evil one, Set, destroyed the sun, i.e. when it did not shine for a few years, they postulated that Osiris was now a dead god, and therefore God of the Dead. He was resurrected in the form of his son Horus - when the sun reappeared. But he himself also remained as the god of the dead.

Greece's Typhon

The Greek also had a similar story. Their chief god, Zeus, battles Typhon. Typhon has been described as the largest, and ugliest monster ever born. He had a hundred horrible heads that touched the stars. Lava and red-hot stones poured from his gaping mouths. He hissed like a hundred snakes and roared like a hundred lions. He tore up whole mountains and threw them at the gods.

Zeus engaged him in a terrible battle and was defeated. Typhon cut out Zeus' tendons and hid them. Zeus' son is able to return the tendons and repairs Zeus, who returns to an even more heated battle that destroyed almost all living creatures on earth.

When Typhon tore up the huge Mont Aetna to hurl at the gods, Zeus struck Typhon with a hundred thunderbolts and the mountain fell back, pinning Typhon beneath.

Typhon is still there, and that's why Aetna still belches fire, lava, and smoke to this day.

Typhon cutting out Zeus' tendons may be analogous to Set dismembering Osiris. More likely, both stories came from a single, more ancient source.

Greece: Homer's Iliad

Homer, sometime before 800 BC, wrote his famous Iliad. It seems clear that he took materials from a very ancient version of the great disaster.

" ... Zeus, from the top of many-deled Olympus, bade Themis gather the gods in council, where on she went about and called them to the house of Zeus."

Poseidon
Why, wielder of the lighting, have you called the gods to council?

Zeus
You know my purpose, shaker of earth and wherefore I have called you hither.

Zeus gave the word for war.

Poseidon shook the vast earth, and bade the high hills tremble.

Hades, King of the realms below was struck with fear; he sprang panic-stricken from his throne and cried aloud in terror lest Poseidon, lord of the earthquake, should crack the ground over his head, and lay bare his moldy mansions to the sight of mortals and immortals - mansions so ghastly grim that even the gods shudder to think of them.

Homer frequently refers to Poseidon as: "earth-encir-cling Poseidon", and states:

Forthwith he shed a darkness before the eyes of the son of Peleus, ...

Peleus was a mortal wedded to Thetas, a sea nymph. Her son was Achilles - the key hero of Iliad.

This may refer to the darkness caused by the cloud of the disaster.

Later Homer tells of the darkness being removed from Achilles eyes.

The author believes that several ancient documents - and rewrites thereof, existed in Homer's time. And just as various scribes, et al rewrote some of these, as well documented in the clay tablets of Sumer and Babylon, so Homer may have done some rewriting.

Unfortunately, most of the ancient records available in Homer's time were destroyed with the destruction of the great library in Alexandria.

Rome's Metamorphoses by Ovid: Phaeton

One of history's most famous writers is the Roman Ovid, more formally known as Publius Ovidius Naso. He lived from 43 BC to 18 AD and wrote his Metamorphoses about 1 AD.

Book II of Metamorphoses is Ovid's description of Phaeton.

Phaeton is the son of Apollo, i.e. the son of the sun. To prove this to his schoolmates, Phaeton asks to drive the sun's chariot for a day. His father responds:

Apollo

I beg you to withdraw this request. It is not a safe boon, nor one, my Phaeton, suited to your youth and strength.

Your lot is mortal, and you ask what is beyond a mortal's power. In your ignorance you aspire to do that which not even the gods themselves may do. None but myself may drive the flaming car of day. Not even Jupiter whose terrible right arm hurls the thunderbolts.

The first part of the way is steep, and such as the horses when fresh in the morning can hardly climb; the middle is high up in the heavens, whence I myself can scarcely, without alarm, look down and behold the earth and sea stretched beneath me. The last part of the road descends rapidly, and requires most careful driving. Tethys, who is waiting to receive me, often trembles for me lest I should fall headlong. Add to all this, the heaven is all the time turning round and carrying the stars with it.

I have to be perpetually on my guard lest that movement, which sweeps everything else along, should hurry me also away. Suppose I should lend you the chariot, what would you do?

Could you keep your course while the sphere was revolving under you?

Perhaps you think that there are forests and cities, the abodes of gods, and palaces and temples on the way.

On the contrary, the road is through the midst of frightful monsters. You pass by the horns of the Bull, in front of the Archer, and near the Lion's jaws, and where the Scorpion stretches its arms in one direction and the Crab in another.

Nor will you find it easy to guide those horses, with their breasts full of fire that they breathe forth from their mouths and nostrils. I can scarcely govern them myself, when they are unruly and resist the reins. Beware, my son, lest I be the donor of a fatal gift; recall your request while yet you may. Do you ask me for a proof that you are sprung from my blood? I give you a proof in my fears for you.

Look at my face - I would that you could look into my breast, you would there see all a father's anxiety. Finally, he continued, look round the world and choose whatever you will of what earth or sea contains most precious- ask it and fear no refusal. This only I pray you not to urge. It is not honour, but destruction you seek. Why do you hang round my neck and still entreat me?

Figure 65: The son of Apollo gets the chance to drive his father's chariot.

> **You shall have it if you persist - the oath is sworn and must be kept - but I beg you to choose more wisely."**

He ended; but the youth rejected all admonition and held to his demand. So, having resisted as long as he could, Apollo at last led the way to where stood the lofty chariot.

It was of gold, the gift of Vulcan; the axle was of gold, the pole and wheels of gold, the spokes of silver. Along the seat were rows of chrysolites and diamonds, which reflected all around the brightness of the sun.

While the daring youth gazed in admiration, the early Dawn threw open the purple doors of the east, and showed the pathway strewn with roses. The stars withdrew, marshaled by the Daystar, which last of all retired also.

The father, when he saw the earth beginning to glow, and the Moon preparing to retire, ordered the Hours to harness up the horses. They obeyed, and led forth from the lofty stalls the Steeds full fed with ambrosia, and attached the reins.

Then the father bathed the face of his son with a powerful unguent, and made him capable of enduring the brightness of the flame. He set the rays on his head, and, with a foreboding sigh, said,

Apollo

If, my son, you will in this at least heed my advice, spare the whip and hold tight the reins.

They go fast enough of their own accord; the labour is to hold them in. You are not to take the straight road directly between the five circles, but turn off to the left. Keep within the limit of the middle zone, and avoid the northern and the southern alike. You will see the marks of the northern and the southern alike. You will see the marks of the wheels, and they will serve to guide you. And, that the skies and the earth may each receive their due share of heat, go not too high, or you will burn the heavenly dwellings, nor too low, or you will set the earth on fire; the middle course is safest and best. And now I leave you to your chance, which I hope will plan better for you than you have done for yourself. Night is passing out of the western gates and we can delay no longer.

Figure 66: Phaeton drove the chariot too close to earth and set the world on fire.

Take the reins; but if at last your heart fails you, and you will benefit by my advice, stay where you are in safety, and suffer me to light and warm the earth.

The agile youth, sprang into the chariot, stood erect, and grasped the reins with delight pouring out thanks to his reluctant parent.

Meanwhile the horses fill the air with their snortings and fiery breath, and stamp the ground impatient. Now the bars are let down, and the boundless plain of the universe lies open before them. They dart forward and cleave the opposing clouds, and outrun the morning breezes which started from the same eastern goal.

The steeds soon perceived that the load they drew was lighter than usual; and as a ship without ballast is tossed hither and thither on the sea, so the chariot, without its accustomed weight, was dashed about as if empty.

They rush headlong and leave the traveled road. He is alarmed, and knows not how to guide them; nor, if he knew, has he the power.

Then, for the first time, the Great and Little Bear were scorched with heat, and would fain, if it were possible, have plunged into the water; and the Serpent which lies coiled up round the north pole, torpid and harmless, grew warm, and with warmth felt its rage revive. Bootes, they say, fled away, though encumbered with his plough, and all unused to rapid motion.

When hapless Phaeton looked down upon the earth, now spreading in vast extent beneath him, he grew pale and his knees shook with terror. In spite of the glare all around him, the sight of his eyes grew dim. He wished he had never touched his father's horses, never learned his parentage; never prevailed in his request.

Figure 67: Phaeton falls to Earth, as illustrated by Peter Paul Rubens in 1605.

He is borne along like a vessel that flies before a tempest, when the pilot can do no more and betakes himself to his prayers.

What shall he do? Much of the heavenly road is left behind, but more remains before. He turns his eyes from one direction to the other; now to the goal whence he began his course, now to the realms of sunset which he is not destined to reach. He loses his self-command, and knows not what to do - whether to draw tight the reins or throw them loose; he forgets the names of the horses.

He sees with terror the monstrous forms scattered over the surface of heaven. Here the Scorpion extended his two great arms, with his tail and crooked claws stretching over two signs of the zodiac. When the boy beheld him, reeking with poison and menacing with his fangs, his course failed, and the reins fell from his hands. The horses, when they felt them loose on their backs, dashed headlong, and unrestrained went off into unknown regions of the sky, in among the stars, hurling the chariot over pathless places, now up in high heaven, now down almost to the earth.

The moon saw with astonishment her brother's chariot running beneath her own. The clouds begin to smoke, and the mountaintops take fire; the fields are parched with heat, the plants wither, the trees with their leafy branches burn, the harvest is ablaze!

But these are small things. Great cities perished, with their walls and towers; whole nations with their people were consumed to ashes! The forest-clad mountains burned, Athos and Taurus and Tmolus and OEte; Ida, once celebrated for fountains, but now all dry; the Muses' mountain Helicon, and Haemus; Aetna, with fires within and without, and Parnassus, with his two peaks, and Rhodope, forced at last to part with his snowy crown. Her cold climate was no protection to

Figure 68: The Italian Naiads survive and come to honor Phaeton.

Scythia, Caucasus burned, and Ossa and Pindus, and, greater than both, Olympus; the Alps high in air, and the Apennines crowned with clouds.

Then Phaeton beheld the world on fire, and felt the heat intolerable. The air he breathed was like the air of a furnace and full of burning ashes, and the smoke was of a pitchy darkness. He dashed forward he knew not whither.

Then, it is believed, the people of Ethiopia became black by the blood being forced so suddenly to the surface, and the Libyan Desert was dried up to the condition in which it remains to this day.

The Nymphs of the fountains, with disheveled hair, mourned their waters, nor were the rivers safe beneath their banks: Tanais smoked, and Caicus, Xanthus, and Meander, Babylonian Euphrates and Ganges, Tagus with golden sands, and Cayster where the swans resort. Nile fled away and hid his head in the desert, and there it still remains concealed. Where he used to discharge his waters through seven mouths into the sea, there seven dry channels alone remained.

The earth cracked open, and through the chinks light broke into Tartarus, and frightened the king of shadows and his queen. The sea shrank up. Where here before was water, it became a dry plain; and the mountains that lie beneath the waves lifted up their heads and became islands. The fishes sought the lowest depths, and the dolphins no longer ventured as usual to sport on the surface.

Even Nereus, and his wife Doris, with the Nereids, their daughters, sought the deepest caves for refuge.

Thrice Neptune essayed to raise his head above the surface, and thrice was driven back by the heat.

Earth, surrounded as she was by waters, yet with head and shoulders bare, screening her face with her hand, looked up to heaven, and with a husky voice

called on Jupiter (Zeus):

Earth

"O ruler of the gods, if I have deserved this treatment, and it is your will that I perish with fire, why withhold your thunderbolts? Let me at least fall by your hand. Is this the reward of my fertility, of my obedient service? Is it for this that I have supplied herbage for cattle, and fruits for men, and frankincense for your altars? But if I am unworthy of regard, what has my brother Ocean done to deserve such a fate?

If neither of us can excite your pity, think, I pray you, of your own heaven, and behold how both the poles are smoking which

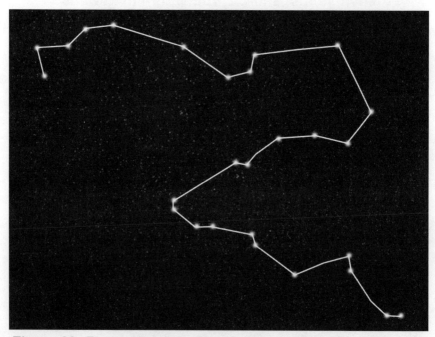

Figure 69: Pennsylvania's Constellation, Eridanus was known as the River Eridanus.

sustain your palace, which must fall if they
be destroyed.

Atlas faints, and scarce holds up his burden.
If sea, earth, and heaven perish, we fall into
ancient Chaos.
Save what yet remains to us from the
devouring flame. O, take thought for our
deliverance in this awful moment!"

Figure 70: Phaeton falls into the heavenly river Eridanus, as
illustrated by Paul Rubens in 1605.

Thus spoke Earth, and overcome with heat and thirst, could say no more.

Then Jupiter omnipotent, calling to witness all the gods, including him who had lent the chariot, and showing them that all was lost unless some speedy remedy were applied, mounted the lofty tower from whence he diffuses clouds over the earth, and hurls the forked lightnings. But at that time not a cloud was to be found to interpose for a screen to earth, nor was a shower remaining unexhausted. He thundered, and brandishing a lightning bolt in his right hand launched it against the charioteer, and struck him at the same moment from his seat and from existence!

Phaeton, with his hair on fire, fell headlong, like a shooting star which marks the heavens with its brightness as it falls, and Eridanus, the great river, received him and cooled his burning frame.

The Italian Naiads reared a tomb for him, and inscribed these words upon the stone:

> *"Driver of Phoebus' (Apollo's) chariot, Phaeton, Struck by Jove's thunder, rests beneath this stone. He could not rule his father's car of fire, Yet was it much so nobly to aspire."*

Figure 71: Ovid credits Phaeton with noble effort.

Hebrew's Satan

The Bible mentions Satan in many places. Perhaps the verses most closely related to the disaster story are from Revelation.

> *And I beheld when he had opened the sixth seal, and lo, there was a great earthquake; and the sun became black as sackcloth of hair, and the moon became as blood; 6:12*

> *And the stars of heaven fell unto the earth ... 6:13*

> *... And every mountain and island were moved out of their places. 6:14*

> *And the Kings of the earth, and .... (everyone) hid themselves in the dens and in the rocks of the mountains. 6:15*

This sounds very much like the disaster described in Chapter Four. And it appears in agreement with other "sacred texts" we have presented.

> *And there was a war in heaven; Michael and his angels fought against the dragon; and the dragon fought and his angels, 12:7*

> *And prevailed not; neither was their place found any more in heaven. 12:8*

*And the great dragon was cast out, that old
serpent, called the Devil, and Satan,
which deceiveth the whole world; he was
cast out into the earth, and his angels were
cast out with him. 12:9*

This certainly sounds like a description of the disaster.
And it may have been taken from recorded documents that
later became the Book of Job. It surely acknowledges who
Satan is:

*That old serpent, called the Devil, and Satan.
12:9*

Isaiah also refers to the crooked serpent and tends to
clarify the definition of the dragons and the leviathan.

*In that day the Lord with his sore and great
and strong sword shall punish leviathan the
piercing serpent; even leviathan that crooked
serpent; and He shall slay the dragon that is
in the sea. 27:1*

This is again discussed in Chapter Eight.

Ute's Ta-Wats

The Ute Indians of California remember when:

"... the sun was shivered into a thousand fragments, which fell to earth causing a general conflagration."

Their hero of the disaster was Ta-Wats who:

"... Fled the burning earth (that) consumed his feet, consumed his legs, consumed his body, consumed his hands and arms - all were consumed but the head alone, which bowled across valleys and over mountains, fleeing destruction from the burning earth, until at last, swollen with heat, the eyes of ... (Ta-Wats)... Burst and the tears gushed forth in a flood which spread over the earth and extinguished the fire."

It seems obvious that this is the same story, but remembered by a simpler people.

The Key Players in the Memories of the Disaster

Country	Satan Name	Hero Name
Sumer	Marduk	Marduk
India	Vritra	Indra
Norse	Fenris-Wolf &	
	Midgard Serpent	Thor
	Hodur	Balder
Persia	Tistrya	
Egypt	Set (Seb)	Osiris
Greece	Typhon	Zeus
		Adonis
	Cacus	Hercules
Rome	Phaeton	
Hebrews	Satan	Jehovah
Brazil	Ariconte	Timandonar
Maya	Serpent Sky God	Hunab Ku
Ute	Ta-Wats	Ta-Wats

Figure 72: The hero and the villian were given different names by the various cultures of antiquity.

Summary Review of The War

So we have many names for the chunk that caused the great disaster, as summarized in the table. And almost everyone recognized it as a great, fiery serpent.

Most of the "memories" are very similar. Only the Sumerians recognized the intruder as a good "God". This is because they made the villain to be the god Tiamat - which disappeared from the heavens.

And, in fact, most of the damage was done by pieces from Tiamat - including her moon Kingu - which exploded and did the most damage.

The Norse had more than one version, because - it is believed - writers continued "editing" and changing the story even beyond 1000 AD.

The Greeks also had several versions, as written by the great writers: Herodotus, Pliny and Strabo.

Other than the ancient Sumerians and Babylonians, most of the others recognized the intruder as an evil serpent, and this became the dominate belief.

There can be little doubt that this intruder was the basis for Satan.

Satan caused the flood.

Figure 73: Excavations in ancient Mesopotamia.

Chapter 7
Ancient Documentation of The Flood and Cold

"The past is never dead. It's not even past."
William Faulkner

There are several ancient documented stories of the flood, and hundreds of oral versions.

It is generally agreed that the story of Ziusudra of ancient Mesopotamia is the oldest written version.

Sumerian Ziusudra

The ancient clay tablets tell how human noise vexed the chief god Enlil so much that he persuaded the divine assembly to vote the destruction of man by sending a flood.

At that time, Ziusudra was king and lustration priest. He fashioned, being a seer, the god of giddiness and stood in awe beside it, wording his wishes humbly.

As he stood there regularly day after day something that was not a dream was appearing:
Conversation.
A swearing of oaths by heaven and earth,
A touching of throats.
And the gods bringing their thwarts up to Kiur.
And as Ziusudra stood there beside it, he went on hearing:

Step up to the wall to my left and listen!
Let me speak a word to you at the wall
and may you grasp what I say,
may you heed my advice!

By our hand a flood will sweep over
the cities of the half-bushel baskets, and the country;
The decision, that mankind is to be destroyed has been made.
A verdict, a command of the assembly cannot be revoked,
An order of An and Enlil is not known ever to have been countermanded,
Their kingship, their term, has been uprooted,

They must bethink themselves of that.
Now...
What I have to say to you...

Here the text has been lost, but other fragments suggest that the lost text instructed Ziusudra to build a chest (boat) to survive the flood. Then:

All the evil winds, all stormy winds gathered
into one,
And with them, then, the flood was sweeping
over the cities of the half-bushel baskets for
seven days and seven nights.
After the flood had swept over the country,
after the evil wind had tossed the big boat
about on the great waters,
the sun came out spreading light
over heaven and earth.

Ziusudra then drilled an opening in the big
boat.
And the gallant Utu (sun) sent his light
into the interior of the big boat.
Ziusudra, being king,
stepped up before Utu kissing the ground
before him.
The king was butchering oxen,
was being lavish with the sheep
Barley cakes, crescents together with...

... he was crumbling for him
juniper, the pure plant of the
mountains, he filled on the fire
and with a ...
clasped to the breast he ...

Here the text is lost. Then:

He will disembark the small animals
that come up from the earth!

Ziusudra, being king, stepped up before An
and Enlil kissing the ground.
And An and Enlil after honoring him were
granting him life like a god's, we're making
lasting breath of life, like a god's, descend into
him.
That day they made Ziusudra, preserver, as
king, of the name of the small animals and the
seed of mankind,
live toward the east over the mountains
in mount Dilmun.

Akkadian Uthnapishtim

Some of the clay tablets also tell a similar story for the Akkadian Uthnapishtim. He was the son of King Ubar-Tutu. The gods became angry because mankind was making too much noise. But the god Ea told the reeds at the riverside so that Uthnapishtim could overhear. The story is almost identical to the Ziusudra story.

Greek Deucalion's Flood: Apollodorus Version

In Greek mythology, the supreme god Zeus, decides to destroy mankind because they were disrespectful and sinful. Prometheus, a man that benefits men (a priest?), warns his son Deucalion that the gods Zeus and Poseidon are going to cause a flood, and tells him to build a boat.

And Prometheus had a son Deucalion. He reigning in the regions about Phthia, married Phyrra, the daughter of Epimetheus and Pandora, the first woman fashioned by the Gods. And when Zeus would destroy the men of the Bronze Age, Deucalion by the advice of Prometheus constructed a chest, and having stored it with provisions he embarked in it with Pyrrha. But Zeus by pouring heavy rain from heaven flooded the greater part of Greece, so that all men were destroyed, except a few who fled to the high mountains in the neighborhood. It was there that the mountains in Thessaly parted, and that all the world outside the Isthmus and Peloponnese was overwhelmed. But Deucalion, floating in the chest over the sea for nine days and as many nights, drifted to Parnassus, and there, when the rain ceased, he landed and sacrificed to Zeus, the god of Escape.

Deucalion's Flood, Ovid's Version

Ovid, the great Roman writer, later gave his version. Only limited excerpts are given for brevity.

> *Jove standing up aloft and leaning on his ivory Mace,*
> *Right dreadfully his bushy locks did thrice or four times shake,*
> *Wherewith he made both Sea and Land and Heaven it self to quake.*

This basically agrees with the other stories that there were earthquakes proceeding the flood.

> *I must destroy both man and beast and all the mortal kind.*
> *The man that had so traitorously against their Lord conspired.*

> *That all had sworn and sold themselves to mischief usto grieve.*
> *And therefore as they all offend: so am I fully bent,*
> *That all forthwith (as they deserve) shall have due punishment.*

So Zeus decides to destroy man, and some of the other gods agreed.

> **These words of Jove some of the Gods did openly approve,**
> **And with their sayings more to wrath his angry courage move.**

And some did give assent by signs. Yet did it grieve them all
That such destruction utterly on all mankind should fall,

To savage beasts to waste and spoil, because of mans offence.
The king of Gods bade cease their thought and questions in that case,
And cast the care thereof on him.

The beasts are also destroyed - because of man's offenses.

Zeus first thinks to destroy with fire, but reconsiders for the following reasons.

And now his lightning had he thought on all the earth to throw,
But that he feared lest the flames perhaps so high should grow ...
As for to set the Heaven on fire, and burn up all the sky.

Zeus also remembers as earlier prophesy, i.e. a "destiny" that is to come in the future, and therefore he cannot use fire as a destruction at this time.

He did remember furthermore how that by destiny
A certain time should one day come, wherein both Sea and Land
And Heaven itself should feel the force of Vulcan's scorching brand,
So that the huge and goodly work of all the world so wide

Should go to wreck, for doubt whereof
forthwith he laid aside.

So Zeus decides to use a flood.

He did determine with himself the mortal kind
to drown. ...

And to the Sea with flowing streams swollen
above their banks,
One rolling in another necke, they rushed
forth by ranks.

Himself with his threatened Mace, did lend the
earth a blow,

That made it shake and open ways for waters
forth to flow.

Men, beasts, trees, corne, and with their gods
were Churches washed away.
No difference was between the sea and
ground,
For all was sea: there was no shore nor
landing to be found.
Some climbed up to tops of hills, and some
rowed to and fro
One over corne and tops of towns, whom
waves did over whelm.
The Sea nymphs wondered under waves the
towns and groves to see,
And Dolphins played among the tops and
boughs of every tree.
The grim and greedy Wolfe did swim among
the siely sheep,

The Lion and the Tiger fierce were borne upon the deep.
The fleeting fowls long having sought for land to rest upon,
Into the Sea with weary wings were driven to fall anon.
Unwonted waves on highest tops of mountains did rebound.
The greatest part of men were drowned, and such as escaped the flood,
Forlorn with fasting overlong did die for want of food.

When at this hill (for yet the Sea had whelmed all beside)
Deucalion and his bedfellow, without all other guide,
Arrived in a little Bark immediately they went,
And to the Nymphs of Corycus with full devout intent
Did honor due, and to the Gods to whom that famous hill
Was sacred, and to Themis eke in whose most holy will
Consisted then the Oracles. In all the world so round
A better nor more righteous man could never yet be found
Than was Deucalion, nor again a woman, maiden nor wife,
That feared God so much as she, nor led so good a life. ...

*When Jove beheld how all the world stood like
a plash of rain,
And of so many thousand men and women did
remain
But one of each, howbeit those both just and
both devout,
He brake the Clouds, and did command that
Boreas with his stout
And sturdy blasts should chase the flood, that
Earth might see the sky.*

*And swelling streams of flowing floods within
her channels sank.
Then hills did rise above the waves that had
them overflow,
And as the waters did decrease the ground did
seem to grow.
The world restored was again, which though
Deucalion rejoiced.*

What very ancient sources did Ovid have? It certainly
describes the flood - and provides details not included in
the other stories.

Such sources were most likely destroyed long ago.
But: we may yet find them in some ancient lost library. We
can only hope.

Figure 74: "And the rain was upon the earth forty days and forty nights". Genesis 7:12

Hebrew Noah's Flood

The best-known story of the flood is the story of Noah in the Book of Genesis in the Bible.

And the Lord said, I will destroy man whom I have created from the face of the earth; both man, and beast, and the creeping thing, and the fowls of the air; for it repenteth me that I have made them. 6:7

But Noah found grace in the eyes of the Lord. 6:8

And God said unto Noah, The end of all flesh is come before me; for the earth is filled with violence through them; and, behold, I will destroy them with the earth. 6:13

Make thee an ark of gopher wood; ... 6:14

In the six hundredth year of Noah's life, in the second month, the seventeenth day of the month, the same day were all the fountains of the great deep broken up, and the windows of heaven were opened. 7:11

And the rain was upon the earth forty days and forty nights. 7:12

And the flood was forty days upon the earth; and the waters increased, and bare up the ark, and it was lift up above the earth. 7:17

And the waters prevailed upon the earth an hundred and fifty days. 7:24

So Genesis tells us that God caused the flood. But Revelation has a different story.

> *And there was war in heaven; Michael and his angels fought against the dragon; and the dragon fought and his angels, 12:7*

> *And prevailed not; neither was their place found any more in heaven. 12:8*

> *And the great dragon was cast out, that old serpent, called the Devil, and Satan, which deceiveth the whole world: he was cast out into the earth, and his angels were cast out with him. 12:9*

Thus Revelation tells us that Satan was thrown to earth and thereby caused the flood.

Putting both stories together tells us that God caused the flood by throwing Satan to earth.

American Ute's Ta-Wat Version

The Ute tribes of America have a very different story of the flood, indicating perhaps a separate memory.

> *(There was a war and) ... The sun was shivered into a thousand fragments, which fell to earth causing general conflagration. Then Ta-Wats fled before the destruction ...*
> *and as he fled the burning earth consumed his feet, consumed his legs, consumed his body, consumed his hands and arms - all were consumed but the head alone, which bowled across valleys and over mountains, fleeing destruction from the burning earth, until at last, swollen with heat, the eyes of ...*
> *Ta-Wats ... Burst and the tears gushed forth in a flood, which spread over the earth and extinguished the fire.*

Here again we have the same story elements:

1. War in heaven;
2. Sun shivered and falls to earth;
3. Earth burns;
4. A flood puts out the fires.

Clearly this is just a different version of the same great disaster.

Norse Edda: Bitter Cold

The Eddas describe the war in heaven, and then refer to the flood, as previously described. Then they speak of the bitter cold.

> *First there is a winter called the Fimbuyl winter, the mighty; the great, the iron winter, when snow drives from all quarters, the frosts are so severe, the winds so keen, that there is no joy in the sun. There are three such winters in succession, without any intervening summer.*
> *... As soon as the streams that ... (flow under the ice) had come so far ... (they) ... turned into ice. And when this ice stopped and flowed no more, then gathered over it the drizzling rain ... And froze into rime, and one layer of ice was laid upon another clear into (their land) and all of (their land) was filled with thick and heavy ice and rime, and everywhere were drizzling rain and gusts.*

Their literature speak of severe, bitter cold that lasted for three years. It is interested to note that Russian literature also state that the winter lasted three years.

160

Persia's Yima: Bitter Cold

Ancient Persia also has a story almost identical to the Norse in their literature. It appears that both are from the same, ancient source.

Mexican Aztecs: Bitter Cold

The Aztecs of Mexico also remember the time of bitter cold, as indicated in their ancient prayer.

> *Know, O Lord.... The men have no garments, nor the women, to cover themselves ...*
> *With great toil and weariness they scrape together enough for each day, going by mountain and wilderness seeking their food; so faint and enfeebled are they that their bowels cleave to their ribs, and; all their body re-echoes with hollowness ...*
> *They tremble with cold, and for leanness they stagger walking ...*
> *Though they stay by a fire, they find little heat.*

The Key Flood Stories

Country	Warned By	Why	Hero
Sumer	Enki	Not serving gods	Ziusudra
Akkadian	Ea	Not serving gods	Uthnapishtim
Greece	Prometheus	Wickedness	Deucalion
Hebrew	Jehovah	Wickedness	Noah
Ute	No one	None	Ta-Wats
Norse			Thor
Persia	Gods		Yima
Egypt	No one	None	Osiris

Figure 75: Each of the many stories share common elements.

Summary Review of The Flood Stories

Memories of the great disaster do indeed exist in almost all parts of our world.

These flood stories are generally considered to be the major ones. There are dozens more.

The worldwide literature is too consistent to be a coincidence. Is seems quite clear that there was indeed a worldwide flood. It seems also, that many of the stories may have derived from a common story. And perhaps there were only a few source stories for the dozens that exist today.

Figure 76: Job in the cave.

Chapter 8
The Eyewitness

"Though the Lord causes grief, yet He will show compassion."

Lamentations 3:32

The Book of Job in the Bible, is the oldest in the world.

This is the belief of major scholars including Magee, Schultens, Lowth and Michaelis.

Job and the Chief Priest Eliphaz, and their companions were eyewitnesses to Noah's Flood. The eyewitness account was written while the group took shelter from the disaster in a cave.

Being mankind's oldest available document, there have been many rewrites and interpretations. This interpretation provides three comparative sets of information:

1. The events as recorded in the King James version of the Bible;
2. The events as determined by the scientific evidence presented in Chapter Four; and
3. The author's interpretation of the Bible's Book of Job in light of the scientific evidence.

To clearly distinguish the Biblical quotes from the other two "opinions", quotes from the Bible are in bold italic and the others are in normal text.

Description of the Disaster

We begin with Job 2:7 because key scholars agree that the first part of the Book of Job is very different than the basic story, and was clearly written much later than the body of the Book.

> *So went Satan forth from the presence of the Lord, and smote Job with sore boils from the sole of his foot unto his crown. 2:7*

Satan, the chunk of material from the supernova, left the heavens and rained hot rocks and sands upon earth. Job and his companions had been watching the approaching Satan for many days. They had begun to experience the heavy winds caused by Satan pulling earth's atmosphere towards it.

Job was outside watching Satan when a great gust of wind bearing hot sands and dust, suddenly began to rain down upon him. Some burned through his clothes and penetrated his skin **"from the sole of his foot unto his crown"**.

Job ran and found shelter in a near-by cave where he had gone to seek shelter from the approaching Satan, which had been visible for many days. He slumped to the ground in great pain from the multitude of burns.

Several companions had also gone to the cave to escape the disaster. During this time, and later, their experiences were written.

One of Job's companions tells him what has happened.

> *The fire of God is fallen from heaven, and hath burned up the sheep, and thy servants, and consumed them.... 1:16*

And, behold, there came a great wind from the wilderness, and smote the four corners of the house, and it fell upon (thy sons and thy daughters) and they are dead.... 1:19

This is clearly a description of the events described in Chapter Four, which describes the scientific evidence of this disaster. Rewrites and attempted clarifications down through the ages - made by scribes, et al who did not witness the events, and who could not imagine such occurrences, have altered the original writing - but the basic story facts are left intact.

One of Job's "priestly" companions, Eliphaz, tries to justify God's action in sending this disaster. In his attempt, he further describes the events.

By the blast of God they perish, and by the breath of his nostrils are they consumed. 4:9

Although affliction cometh not forth of the dust, neither doth trouble spring out of the ground; 5:6

Yet man is born unto trouble as the sparks fly upward. 5:7

"As the sparks fly upward" has been translated by scholars Maurer and Gesenius from the available Hebrew documents to say "As the sons of lighting fly high". That is, the disaster - the trouble - does not come from earth, but from above - from the heavens.

Eliphaz continues in his attempts to convince Job that God has His own reasons for this disaster, and that man should not question God.

> *I would seek unto God, and unto God would I commit my cause; 5:8*

> *Which doeth great things, and unsearchable marvelous things without number. 5:9*

Eliphaz gives examples of what God can do. He describes good things and bad things - such as this disaster.

> *They meet with darkness in the daytime, and grope in the noonday as in the night. 5:14*

Job Complains of the Injustis

The sun has now been blotted out by the smoke and debris for a long time.

And Eliphaz continues in his attempts to justify God's purposes and actions. But Job, in great pain from his burns, is not yet in the mood to hear someone try to justify God's actions. He believes he personally has done more good than bad.

> *Oh that my grief were thoroughly weighed, and my calamity laid in the balances together! 6:2*
>
> *For the arrows of the Almighty are within me, the poison whereof drinkth up my spirit; the terrors of God do set themselves in array against me. 6:4*

He is lamenting of his wounds, and the poisons festering in his burns. He prefers death to this suffering.

> *Oh that I might have my request; and that God would grant me the thing I long for! 6:8*
>
> *Even that it would please God to destroy me; that he would let loose his hand and cut me off. 6:9*
>
> *What is my strength that I should hope? And what is mine end, that I should prolong my life? 6:11*

He points out what is happening to their people, as a result of the disaster. He speaks of ice in his semi-tropical country. And he speaks of the heat. Then laments the faith of his people.

> **The paths of their way are turned aside; they go to nothing and perish. 6:18**

And Job continues in his rebuff to his friend's words.

> **Teach me, and I will hold my tongue; and cause me to understand wherein I have erred. 6:24**

Job turns sarcastic.

> **How forcible are right words! But what doth your arguing reprove? 6:25**

He looks around him - at the cave in which they have taken refuge.

> **Yea, ye overwhelm the fatherless, and, ye dig a pit for your friend. 6:27**

> **Is there not an appointed time to man upon earth? Are not his days also like the days of a hireling? 7:1**

He wonders when the suffering will end.

> **When I lie down, I say, when shall I arise, and the night be gone? 7:4**

He has been in the cave for a long time. The smoke and debris outside has blocked the sun's rays. There is no "day". He wonders when the Night will be gone.

He paints us a picture of his grave, pitiful position.

> *My flesh is clothed with worms and clods of dust; my skin is broken and become loathsome. 7:5*

> *My days... are spent without hope. 7:6*

Job's anger shows.

> *Therefore I will not refrain my mouth; I will speak in the anguish of my spirit; I will complain in the bitterness of my soul. 7:11*

He is miserable, disgusted. He believes he has been treated unfairly. He is angry. He wonders what he has done that was so bad as to deserve this. Why can't he be forgiven for whatever it was?

> *And why dost Thou not pardon my transgression and take away mine iniquity? For now shall I sleep in the dust; and Thou shall seek me in the morning, but I shall not be. 7:21*

He truly feels helpless in his cave while the disaster continues outside. He believes he will die in the cave.

Job's companion, Bildad tries to affirm God's justice. Job answers with questions.

> *I know it is so of a truth; but how should man be just with God? 9:2*

How can man be just with a God that does terrible things?

He describes the terrible things of which God did.

> **Which removeth the mountains, and they know not; which overturneth them in his anger; 9:5**

> **Which shaketh the earth out of her place, and the pillars thereof tremble; 9:6**

> **Which commandeth the sun, and it riseth not; and sealeth up the stars; 9:7**

> **Which alone spreadeth out the heavens, and treadeth upon the waves of the sea. 9:8**

Here Job has described the earthquakes and volcanic actions, and the great pall of smoke and debris that blocks out the sun for a very long time, and the great waves of sea water that sweep the land.

And Job continues.

> **Behold, He taketh away, who can hinder Him? Who will say unto Him, what doest Thou? 9:12**

That is, who can stop God? And who can question God?

> **If God will not withdraw His anger, the proud helpers do stoop under Him. 9:13**

That is, if He will not withdraw his anger from the innocent and obedient:

How much less shall I answer Him, and choose out my words to reason with Him? 9:14

Job continues his questionings, and then describes the bad things God has done to him.

For He breaketh me with a tempest, and multiplied my wounds without cause. 9:17

He will not suffer me to take my breath, but filleth me with bitterness. 9:18

Job continues his questioning argument and draws some conclusions.

This is one thing, therefore I said it: He destroyed the perfect and the wicked. 9:22

He is accusing God of being angry and non-caring, of taking lives of everyone, even the perfect and innocent.

God Gives Earth to Satan

He believes God has given the earth over to Satan.

> *If the scourge slay suddenly, he will laugh at the trial of the innocent. 9:23*

The scourge is the body from heaven: Satan. Satan is causing the great disaster.

> *The earth is given into the hand of the wicked... 9:24*

That is, he believes God has given the earth over to Satan. He asks:

> *... is this not so? If not, where, and who is he? 9:24*

Job Tries to Reason with God

Job now believes that his questioning and open statements against God will surely condemn him.

> *I know (now) that Thou wilt not hold me innocent. 9:26*

And Job believes that no matter what he does, God will punish him.

> *Yet shall Thou plunge me in the ditch, and mine own clothes shall abhor me. 9:31*

God has placed him in this ditch-like cave of filth. And there is no way for him to communicate effectively with God.

> *For He is not a man, as I am, that I should answer Him, and we should come together in judgment. 9:32*

And Job continues to point out that there is also no one to act as a go-between. So Job despairs and pleas for the mercy of God.

> *My soul is weary of my life; I will leave my complaint upon myself; I will speak in the bitterness of my soul. 10:1*

> *I will say unto God, do not condemn me; show me wherefore Thou contendest with me. 10:2*

He asks God to tell him what he has done? He continues in this vein, and then asks:

> *Are not my days few? Cease then, and let me*
> *alone, that I may take comfort a little. 10:20*
>
> *Before I go whence I shall not return, even to*
> *(this) the land of darkness and the shadow of*
> *death. 10:21*
>
> *A land of darkness, as darkness itself; and of*
> *the shadow of death, without any order, and*
> *where the light is as darkness. 10:22*

Job argues that, since his remaining days are few, perhaps he should leave the cave and face the blackness of
chaos outside the cave - and thus end his miserable life.

His companion, Zophas, is fearful for his soul and
believes that he, Zophas, should chastise Job for such
words.

> *And when thou mockest (God), shall no man*
> *make thee ashamed? 11:3*
>
> *If He cut off, and shut up, or gather together,*
> *then who can hinder Him? 11:11*

Zophas is telling Job that they cannot prevent God from
doing God's will. But perhaps:

> *If thou prepare thine heart, and stretch out*
> *thine hands towards Him... 11:13*

Then maybe it will soon all be over.

Because thou shalt forget thy misery, and remember it as waters that pass away. 11:16

And thine age shall be clearer than noonday; thou shalt shine forth, thou shalt be as the morning. 11:17

That is, it will be over, this age of darkness, and then morning will return.

And thou shalt be secure, because there is hope; yea, thou shalt dig about thee, and thou shalt take rest in safety. 11:18

That is, the great tempest will pass. The waters will pass away, then we will dig ourselves out of this cave and find a safe place for rest.

Job is the Son of the King

It is obvious that Job's companions include the holy men of his time. That is why they keep defending God against Job's remarks.

The Holy men of that time were also the keepers of the great knowledge of the civilization and religion, and this positions Job's response.

> *No doubt but ye are the people, and wisdom shall die with you. 12:2*
>
> *But I have understanding as well as you; I am not inferior to you; yea, who knoweth not such things as these. 12:3*

So Job scolds the "Priests" for chastising him.

It should perhaps be noted at this point just who Job and his companions were.

The Arabians declare that Job's father was the founder of the Arabian peoples. Job then, was most likely the son of the King. That is perhaps why he was rescued and taken to the cave; and why "priests" were with him.

It also helps explain Job's stance, his comments and arguments, and the pro-god arguments of his companions.

God is Not Just

Job continues his arguments, noting that the priests - these wise men - his companions - "pretend" that God has only destroyed and made the wicked suffer. He argues if they believe that the sins of men have brought this disaster, go ask the innocent beasts and birds.

> *But ask now the beasts, and they shall teach thee; and the fowls of the air, and they shall tell thee. 12:7*
>
> *Or speak to the earth and it shall teach thee; and the fishes of the sea shall declare unto thee. 12:8*

Job continues in this vein, and then acknowledges the ancient knowledge of the priests.

> *With the ancient is wisdom; and in length of days understandings. 12:12*

This "length of days" refers to the knowledge of the movements of the Gods (planets and stars).
But look what God is doing now.

> *Behold, He breaketh down, and it cannot be built again; He shutteth up a man, and there can be no opening. 12:14*
>
> *Behold, He withholdeth the waters and they dry up. Also He sendeth them out, and they overturn the earth. 12:15*

This summarizes some of the events described in Chapter Four.

*He discovereth deep things out of the
darkness, and bringeth out to light the
shadow of death. 12:22*

That is, God brought something out of the darkness of
the heavens, and these "deep things" brought death.
The priests call it Satan.

*He taketh away the heart of the Chief of the
people of the earth and causeth them to
wander in a wilderness where there is no
way. 12:24*

He may be referring here to the death of his father the
King. In any event, he is referring to the death of their
leader.

*They grope in the dark without light, and He
maketh them to stagger like a drunken man.
12:25*

Job speaks of the people that have left their shelters
after the great waves have swept across the land. Job
probably also looked outside the cave but was too weak to
go out with any of them. It is also likely that some of the
people that went outside returned to report to Job and the
priests.

*Lo, mine eye hath seen all this, mine ear have
heard and understood it. 13:1*

*What ye know, the same do I know also. I am
not inferior unto you. 13:3*

Job obviously resents the priests "talking down to him".

Job Again Tries to Reason with God

> *Surely I would speak to the Almighty, and I desire to reason with God. 13:3*

Job wants to talk with, and reason with God, as opposed to the priests' position of simple faith in God doing His will.

> *But ye are forgers of lies; ye are all physicians of no value. 13:4*

> *Oh that ye would altogether hold your peace! 13:5*

Job, who has probably been taught to respect the priests' wisdom in religious matters, no longer sees reason for such respect. He, in effect, tells them to shut up!

> *Hold your peace, let me alone, that I may speak, and let come on me what will. 13:13*

Job wants the priests to stop justifying God's terrible actions and to stop trying to stifle him in fear that God will destroy his soul.

> *... If I hold my tongue, I shall give up the ghost. 13:19*

> *But man dieth, and wasteth away. Yea, man giveth up the ghost, and where is he? 14:10*

Then Job asks for God's mercy.

*Oh that Thou wouldest hide me in the grave,
that Thou wouldest keep me a secret, until
Thy wrath be past. 14:13*

Job asks God to let him die - to then forget him until
His anger has passed and He is ready to let Job live again.

If a man die, shall he live again? 14:14

Job tells God he will be ready when He calls for him.
Then he provides more insight into the disaster, which, for
brevity, is not repeated here.
Then Eliphaz again rebuffs Job.

*Should a wise man utter vain knowledge,
and fill his belly with east wind
(nonsense). 15:2*

*Should he reason with unprofitable talk?
Or with speeches wherewith he can do no
good? 15:3*

And Eliphaz continues to scold Job. And Job answers.

*I have (now) heard many such things.
Miserable comforters are ye all! 16:2*

Job basically dismisses all their comments and arguments. Then Job discusses - in an analogist manner - what
bad things God is doing to him, and concludes:

*God hath delivered me to the ungodly, and
has turned me over into the hands of the
wicked. 16:11.*

Satan.

Job continues to bemoan what God had done to him, and then resigns himself with:

> ***My friends scorn me. 16:20***

At this point it appears that Job breaks down, crying.

> ***My friends scorn me: but mine eye poureth out tears unto God. 16:20***

And then Job rambles on, complaining and - in a manner of speech - making amends with God.

> ***And where is now my hope? As for my hope, who shall see it? 17:15***

> ***They shall go down to the bars of the pit, when our rest together is in the dust. 17:16***

Job believes there is no hope - and no one to know of hope - and at best, they'll be found in the cave long after they are dead.
Bildad has heard enough. He interrupts.

> ***How long will it be ere ye make an end of words? 18:2***

That is, when will you shut up?
Then Bildad goes into another religious speech, describing the fate of the wicked.
Then Job tires of Bildad's speech.

> ***How long will ye vex my soul, and break me in pieces with words? 19:2***

Job gives another speech and then speaks of his condition.

> *My bone cleaveth to my skin and to my flesh, and I am escaped with the skin of my teeth. 19:20*

> *Have pity upon me, have pity upon me, o ye my friends, for the hand of God hath touched me. 19:21*

They are starving - just skin and bones. Job asks his companions to go easy on him - he is the one with the festering wounds.

Job Wants a Written Record

Then he makes three very important statements.

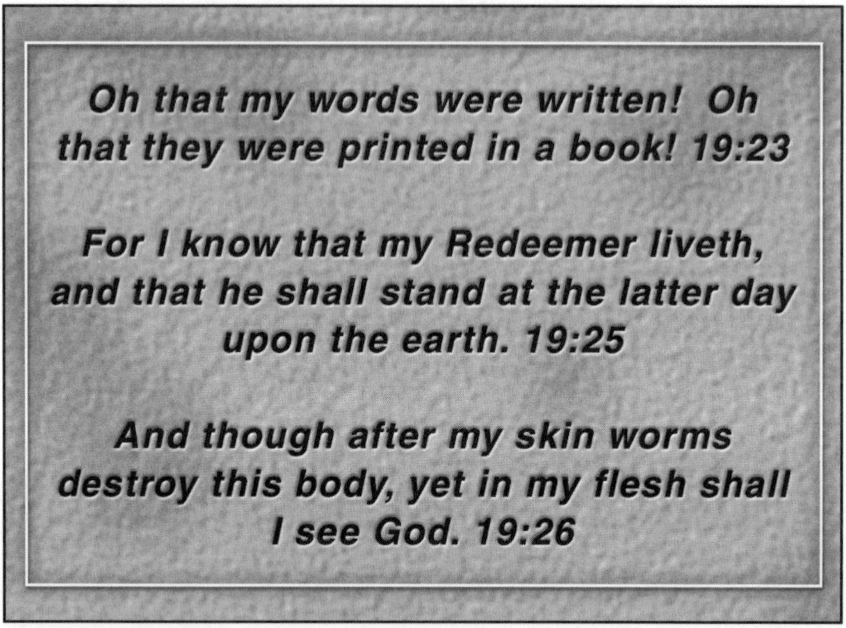

> ***Oh that my words were written! Oh that they were printed in a book! 19:23***
>
> ***For I know that my Redeemer liveth, and that he shall stand at the latter day upon the earth. 19:25***
>
> ***And though after my skin worms destroy this body, yet in my flesh shall I see God. 19:26***

Figure 77: Even with his ordeal, Job knows he will be with God. Job wants a record of the ordeal to be written.

Job acknowledges God and wants the discussion here in the cave, including details of the disaster, to be written down. This desire on his part is probably why we have this extraordinary account of the disaster.

Their discussions and arguments continue. Eliphaz tries to convince Job that he has not been that good to his people.

> ***Thou hast not given water to the weary to drink, and thou hast withholden bread from the hungry. 22:7***

That is, Job, as a rich man did not do all he could have done for the poor.

And besides, God may not know what is going on now, i.e. how bad it is now:

> *Is not God in the height of heaven? And behold the height of the stars, how high they are! 22:12*

> *Can He judge through the dark cloud? 22:13*

> *Thick clouds are a covering to Him, that He seeth not. 22:14*

Job then responds and complains of God's indifference to wickedness. He observes that God seems to treat the good and bad equally.

Bildad then denies that man can be justified with God. And Job agues back. A section of Job's arguments are particularly informative re the disaster.

> **Hell is naked before Him, and destruction hath no covering. 26:6**

God has released hell on earth.

> *He stretcheth out the north over the empty place, and hangeth the earth upon nothing. 26:7*

The chunk came from the north, and now earth has been set loose from its position in the heavens, and among the sun, moon, and stars.

> *He bindeth up the waters in his thick clouds; and the cloud is not rent under them. 26:8*

Here he describes his version of the events described in Chapter Four where much of earth's water is evaporated up into heavy dense clouds, but the waters are not released as rain. It may be recalled from Chapter Four that there was still too much heat for the clouds to condense and fall as rain. The rains occurred later when the earth cooled and the clouds could condense - as described in Chapter Four.

> *He holdeth back the face of his throne, and spreadeth his cloud upon it 26:9*

> *He has compassed the waters with bounds, until the day and night come to an end. 26:10*

The clouds cover the sun and heaven, and there is no night or day - just darkness.

> *The pillars of heaven tremble, and are astonished at his reproof. 26:11*

> *He divideth the sea with his power, and by His understanding He smiteth through the proud. 26:12*

> *By His Spirit He hath garnished the heavens; his hand hath formed the crooked serpent. 26:13*

He caused earthquakes and earth crust shifts and volcanic eruptions. He caused the sea to "pile up" and much of it to evaporate. He killed almost all life. He smashed Tiamat and spread bodies of fire across the heavens - before the clouds formed. And most importantly, He formed the swarm of matter that rushed earth in its undulating path as described in Chapter Three and Four.

This undulating "crooked serpent" was Satan.

Job is ready to Give Up

Job rambles on and talks of the wicked. Did they cause this? And he speaks of man's quest for understanding; and he recalls his former glory as the King's son.

> *Oh that I were as in months past, as in the days when God preserved me. 29:2*

> *When His candle shined upon my head. 29:3*

> *The young men saw me, and hid themselves; and the aged arose, and stood up. 29:8*

And he continues, describing his position, his power, and the good deeds he did for his people. And then he speaks of the present condition of his people.

> *For want and famine they were solitary, fleeing into the wilderness in former time desolate and waste. 30:3*

> *Who cut up mallows by the bushes, and juniper roots for their meat. 30:4*

> *They were driven forth from among men... 30:5*

> *To dwell in the cliffs of the valleys, in the caves of the earth, and in the rocks. 30:6*

During the early part of the disaster, solitary individuals, and small groups such as Job and his companions, ran for the cliffs, rocks, and caves to escape death. Those that didn't were destroyed. The only food they could find in the early darkness was roots and scattered plant parts. They probably also found some dead animals parts.

Job talks of his loss of leadership. His inability to help his people, and his new low position. And then:

> *... The days of affliction have taken hold upon me. 30:16*

> *He have cast me into the mire, and I am become like dust and ashes. 30:19*

God has sent the fire that burned his body, and forced him into this filthy cave.

> *I cry unto Thee, and Thou dost not hear me. I stand up and Thou regardest me not. 30:20*

> *Thou art become cruel to me. 30:21*

And Job cannot understand why God is being so cruel to him. Job believes he has only done good things.

> *Was not my soul grieved for the poor? 30:25*

But look what God has done to me.

> *When I looked for good, then evil came upon me. And when I waited for light, there came darkness. 30:26*

Job just cannot understand why this is all happening. He continues his questioning and arguments.

He is then followed by the younger Elihu who makes the following points.

I am young, and ye are very old; wherefore I... durst not show you mine opinion. 32:6

But now:

I will answer... (And) show mine opinion. 32:17

Wherefore, Job, I pray thee, hear my speeches. 33:1

... God is greater than man. 33:12

Why dost thou strive against Him? For He giveth not account of any of His matters. 33:13

And Elihyu thus reproves Job and justifies God, and extols God's greatness.

Figure 78: God speaks to Job.

God Speaks

The entire style of writing then changes with God speaking directly to Job.

It seems clear, as many Biblical scholars agree, that this latter part of the Book of Job was rewritten in much more recent times.

It still contains phrases relating to the disaster and its aftermath - but apparently the latter writer did not understand the context, and the resulting rewrite appears to be an attempt to "resolve the conflict", as is the traditional custom for writing the end of fictional stories.

Some examples of God speaking to Job, making the point that God is greater than Job, are obviously rewrites of the disaster in that they contain key elements of the disaster.

Where wast thou when I laid the foundations of the earth? 38:4

Do you know:

Where is the way where light dwelleth? 38:19

Hast thou entered into the treasures of the snow? Or hast thou seen the treasures of the hail? 38:22

Hath the rain a father? Or who hath begotten the drops of dew? 38:28

And God refers to the disaster:

Out of whose womb came the ice? And the hoary frost of heaven, who hath gendered it? 38:29

Here the new writer has God show Job His greatness and uniqueness by asking these questions - but note that the questions retain their context of the disaster: snow, hail, ice, hoary frost, etc. This seems to refer to the great cold that followed the disaster.

It appears that Job and his companions continued to write about this phase of the aftermath, and it was edited and rewritten in this manner with God speaking directly to Job.

And then the new writer has Job respond to God's statements.

I know that Thou canst do everything. 42:2

Therefore have I uttered that which I under stood not. 42:3

But now I seeth, I understand, and...

... Wherefore I abhor myself, and repent in dust and ashes. 42:6

And so God forgives Job and orders his companions to make animal sacrifices for Job. God restores Job's prosperity and:

... Lived Job a hundred and 40 years... 42:16

So it is quite clear that later scribes, et al did not understand this very ancient document.

But in spite of their lack of understanding and mistranslations, we can clearly see that the Book of Job is an eyewitness account of the events of the great disaster described in Chapter Four.

We will never know what truly happened to Job - because later editors gave a happy, if almost impossible, ending to Job's story.

But we have the voice of Job, bold, defiant, unshrinking, protesting the cruelty of nature - of God - and appealing from God's awful deed to the sense of justice.

> *We have mankind's oldest surviving written document - a ringside seat to, arguably, the greatest event in man's history!*

Figure 79: The Book of Job is the oldest surviving written document.

Figure 80: Ancient clay tablet of the flood.

Chapter 9
Other Ancient References

"To read is to voyage through time."

Carl Sagan

Many other ancient documents and parts of the Bible also refer to the great disaster.

The Mountain Cave

It is interesting to note that a somewhat similar story to that of Job was found in Sumerian clay tablets. These tablets were written - most likely edited and copied from more ancient documents - over 4000 years ago. It may be that both Job and the Sumerian story were derived from an original document written even earlier.

The Sumerian story could, of course, be about a different person that also hid in a mountain cave to escape the disaster. See which you think is the case.

Only brief excerpts are presented here.

> *The ruling god, Enlil, son of Utu (the sun), "riding on a storm…. Stepped down from heaven to the great earth. His head shines with brilliance, the barbed arrows flash past him like lightning …"*

This sounds like the chunk of material others called Satan.

> *In the great mountains, a sickness befell Lugalbanda. His brother and friends try to make him comfortable in a cave. Later, believing Lugalbanda will die, they leave him in the mountain cave.*

Sounds like Lugalbanda's companions finally escaped the cave and left him there to die.

Later the sun shines through the clouds and Lugalbanda awakens.

*When he lifted his eyes to heaven to Utu (the sun), he wept to him as if to his own father.
In the mountain cave he raised to him his fair hands:*

Lugalbanda
"Utu, I greet you! Let me be ill no longer!

Don't make me eat saltpeter as if it were barley!

Don't make me fall like a throw stick somewhere in the desert unknown to me!

Let me not come to an end in the mountains like a weakling"

Utu accepted his tears. He sent down his divine encouragement to him in the mountain cave.

And all ended well.
This seems very similar to the events described in the Book of Job.

Revelation

Revelation makes some very interesting comments that appear to relate to the disaster and the interpretations by the eyewitnesses.

> *And I saw in the right hand of Him that sat on the throne a book written within and on the backside, sealed with seven seals. 5:1*

Did the writer find an old book of ancient sacred documents?

> *And I beheld when he had opened the sixth seal, and lo, there was a great earthquake; and the sun became black as sackcloth of hair, and the moon became as blood; 6:12*
>
> *And the stars of heaven fell unto the earth.... 6:13*
>
> *... And every mountain and island were moved out of their places. 6:14*
>
> *And the Kings of the earth, and ... (everyone) hid themselves in the dens and in the rocks of the mountains. 6:15*

This sounds very much like an interpretation of Job and his companions writing their observations while they hid in their cave.

This next section appears in agreement with other "sacred texts" we have presented.

And there was a war in heaven; Michael and his angels fought against the dragon; and the dragon fought and his angels, 12:7

And prevailed not; neither was their place found any more in heaven. 12:8

And the great dragon was cast out, that old serpent, called the Devil, and Satan, which deceiveth the whole world; he was cast out into the earth, and his angels were cast out with him. 12:9

This certainly sounds like a description of the disaster. And it may have been taken from recorded documents that later became the Book of Job. It surely acknowledges who Satan is:

... that old serpent, called the Devil, and Satan... 12:9

Psalms

God's actions in relation to the disaster are also described in Psalms, when David is recalling His deeds of old.

> *For God is my King of old, working salvation in the midst of the earth. 74:12*
>
> *Thou didst divide the sea by thy strength. Thou brakest the heads of the dragons in the waters. 74:13*
>
> *Thou brakest the heads of leviathan in pieces, and gavest him to be meat to the people inhabiting the wilderness. 74:14*
>
> *Thou didst cleave the fountain and the flood; Thou driedst up mighty rivers. 74:15*

The dragons and the leviathan are believed to be the various pieces of the swarm of materials that caused the disaster, as described in Chapter Four.

Isaiah

This definition of the dragons and the leviathan is clarified in Isaiah.

> *In that day the Lord with his sore and great and strong sword shall punish leviathan the piercing serpent; even leviathan that crooked serpent; and He shall slay the dragon that is in the sea. 27:1*

It is believed that this says that God will protect Israel in the future as He did in the past - when He destroyed the crooked serpent, i.e. Satan, the cause of the disaster. The destroyed dragon is believed to still be in the sea where some saw (part of) him fall. When he returns from the sea, God "shall slay the dragon that is in the sea."

Bits and pieces of the ancient documentation of the great disaster are found all over the world.

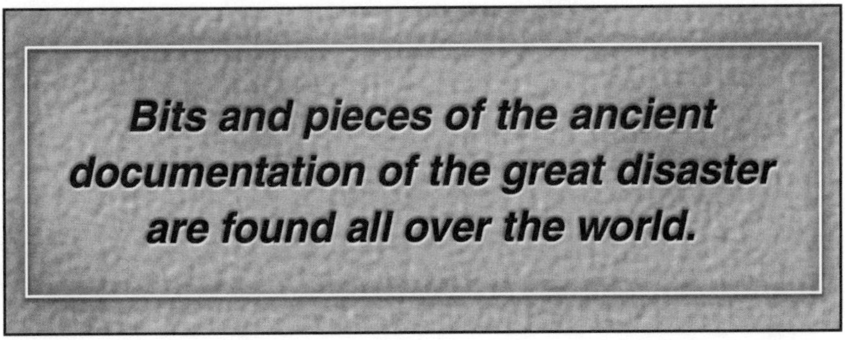

Figure 81: The worldwide disaster was recorded in all parts of the world.

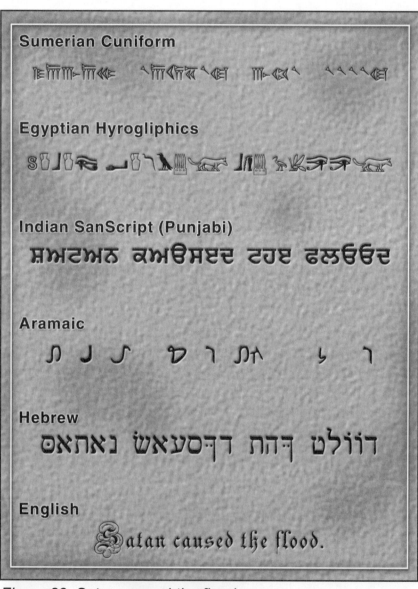

Figure 82: Satan caused the flood.

204

Chapter 10
Conclusions: Where, When, Why

"I could prove God statistically."

George Gallup

So what can we conclude from these ancient documents and all the scientific evidence?

The fabled worldwide flood really did happen.

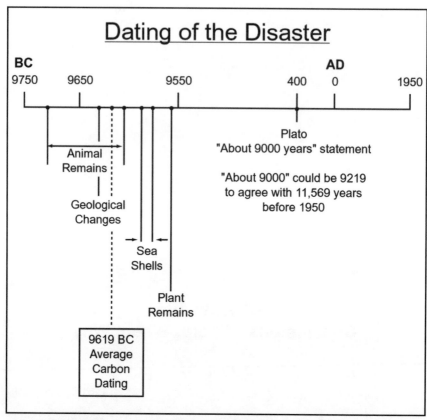

Figure 83: The disaster occurred in April, 9619 BC.

When

It happened about 11,569 years ago.

Carbon dating masses of plant materials buried by the disaster yields an average date of 11,517 years ago. This is 11,517 years before 1950, which was chosen in 1962 to be the baseline for referencing carbon dating.

Similar dating of buried animal deposits yields an average date of 11,670 years ago for the "old world" and 11,564 for the "new world", principally the United States and Canada.

Two separate datings of displaced and buried sea shells indicate average dates of 11,533 and 11,541 years ago.

Major geological displacements have been dated in the old world as occurring at an average of 11,582 years ago.

Averaging all of these dates yield an average of 11,569 years ago.

Plato said that Atlantis was destroyed in the great disaster about 9,000 years before his time, which was about 400 BC. Thus his statement converts to about 11,350 years before 1950.

If Plato's "About 9,000 years ago" were taken as 9,219 years ago, his date would coinside with the average of the sets of carbon dating.

Thus the best date that we can deduce from available data is 11,569 years prior to the reference year 1950.

We therefore take the year of the disaster as 9619 BC.

The time of year can be determined even more precisely. There were large numbers of newborn animals buried in the disaster, which indicated spring or early summer.

Plant remains found in the stomachs of the Siberian mammoths frozen in the disaster and in the plant materials buried in the disaster, show that early summer was the season of the disaster.

In the ancient Persian story of the disaster, it is record-ed that the disaster occurred in the zodiacal constellation of Cancer. This would have been the month of April.

Therefore April of 9619 BC was selected as the most likely date for the disaster.

Plant Materials Burried by the Disaster

Uganda	Denmark	England	Ethiopia
Germany	Italy	Japan	Libya
Lithuania	Netherlands	Norway	Poland
Zimbabwe	Siberia	Switzerland	Alaska
Australia	Canada	New Guinea	New Zealand
Arizona	California	New Mexico	Indiana
Iowa	Michigan	Minnesota	New York
Wisconsin	Wyoming	Ohio	South Dakota
Massachusetts			

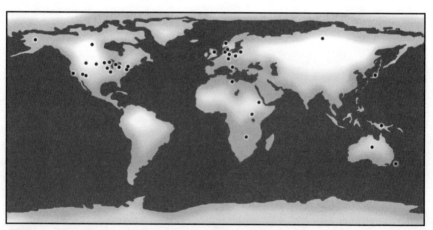

Figure 84: Satan burried plant materials over most of the Earth.

Where

The flood covered the entire earth, except for some of the high mountains.

Impact and debris deposits show that Satan's path was from the northwest to the southeast.

Plant and animal materials were burried on most of the earth.

Animal Materials Buried by the Disaster

Kenya	Spain	Sweden	Greenland
Iceland	India	Scotland	England
France	Germany	Norway	Siberia

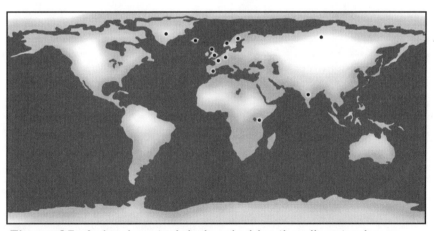

Figure 85: Animal materials burried by the disaster have been found over much of the Earth.

Geographical Changes Occurred Over Most of the Earth

Norway	Iran	Tunisia	Brazil
Canada	Chad	Afar	Hoggar
Ethiopia	Denmark	Taiwan	India
Scotland	Sweden	Siberia	Australia
Chile	New Zealand	Alaska	California
Colorado	Michigan	Nevada	New York
Oregon	Wyoming	Utah	New Mexico
Texas			

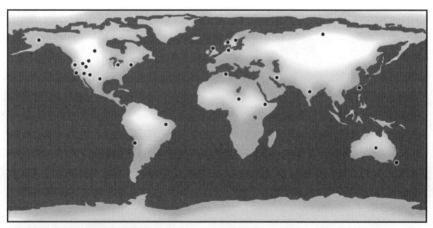

Figure 86: The disaster caused major geological changes over most of the Earth.

Artic Region:

Fossil evidence in the Arctic regions show convincing evidence of great changes in land elevations: some land submersed and some rose significantly in elevation.

The existing drainage systems were almost all completely changed.

There were large lateral crustal displacements, crustal tilting, and over-thrusting of older over younger strata.

Major fissures and fractures occurred - and many still exist.

The Americas:

Most of the Americas greatly increased in elevation. However Florida, the east coast, Honduras and some of the Caribbean area subsided.

There was great volcanic activity in most of the Americas.

North Atlantic:

Similar events occurred in the North Atlantic Region. There was a significant sinking of the Appalachia Mountains.

Some of the lands of Greenland also sank.

Land around the Azores sank beneath the ocean.

Plato records that this was the sinking of Atlantis.

Significant volcanism occurred in the Azores.

Europe:

Similar events also occurred in most of Europe. Most of Europe experienced significant changes in elevations. Great fissures and fractures opened in The British Isles, Irish Sea, the North Sea, and in Norway and the Ural Mountains.

Asia:

Most of the mountains of Asia increased in elevation, however some areas sank.

Africa:

Much of Africa increased in elevation. Lake levels and the basic drainage system was changed.

Pacific Region:

Most of the areas in the Pacific Region, except for the Mindanao Islands, sank. The Mindanao Islands increased in elevation.

Australia and Oceania:

Some of Indonesia and much of the area increased in elevation while much of Indonesia, the Indian Ocean, and some of the other nearby areas sank.

Most of the area experienced increased volcanism. Many land bridges and landmasses disappeared completely.

Where Summary

The carbon dated deposits of plant and animal materials that coincide with the same dates for major worldwide geological changes clearly prove that there was a worldwide disaster that struck Earth in about 9619 BC.

Analysis of the debris deposits and their locations allow us to calculate the trajectory of the "intruder" and the explosion of one of the large bodies orbiting about the intruder; i.e. Tiamat's moon Kinju.

From these analyses it is clear that the great disaster and the following flood occurred over all of the Earth - just as stated in the Bible.

> *"And the waters prevailed exceedingly upon the Earth; and all the high hills, that were under the whole heaven, were covered."*
> *Genesis 7:19*

The great disaster destroyed almost all life on Earth. Many complete species such as the Wooly Mammoth and Saber-Tooth Tiger became extinct.

The entire Earth and all its life forms were forever changed by Satan's visit.

The heavy debris and water-laden clouds completely blocked out the Sun for at least 3 years. There was total darkness.

Eventually scattered sunrays began to break through the thinning clouds, but it was decades before anything like a full day-night cycle returned to Earth.

We now know the When and Where of the great disaster because it was so very well recorded in the debris fields, great terrestrial scars and geological changes that it left us.

And the memory of the great disaster has been well recorded in the folklore, legends, "myths", and written records, some of which have been presented herein.

We know that the great disaster really did happen. And we well know when and where it happened.

It occurred all over the Earth beginning in about April 9619 BC.

When the ancient societies recorded this great disaster, they not only left us with the when and where information, they also gave us their version of why.

Sumerian Cuniform

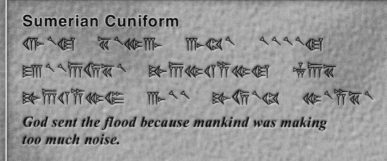

God sent the flood because mankind was making too much noise.

Hebrew

דְּסְעַאשְׁדְּב דוולט דְּהת תנדְּס דוֹג
סְסְדְּנדְּדְּכשְׁדְרו דְּהת תאהת ואס דְּה
תאדְּרג סאו נאם טוֹ

God sent the flood because he saw that the wickedness of man was great.

Roman

PhAETON SON OF APOLLO CAUSED THE
GREAT DISASTER BY RACING THE CHARIOT
OF THE SUN TOO CLOSE TO EARTH

Phaeton, son of Apollo caused the great disaster by, racing the chariot of the Sun too close to earth.

This Book

God caused the disaster by sending parts of the Vela Supernova, i.e. Satan past Earth.

Figure 87: The "why" of the flood.

Why

To understand Why, let's review the ancient documentation.

The oldest record of the disaster, written long before the beginning of the Hebrews and their religion, was incorporated in the Hebrew Bible as the Book of Job.

In the Book of Job, God brags of Job's loyalty and Satan responds:

> *But put forth thine hand now, and touch all that he hath, and he will curse thee to thy face. Job 1:11*

> *And the Lord said unto Satan, Behold, all that he (Job) hath is in thy power..."*
> *Genesis 1:12*

So, according to this oldest written account, Satan causes the great disaster to tempt Job to curse God.

Genesis, however, tells us that:

> *And God said unto Noah, the end of all flesh is come before me; for the Earth is filled with violence through them; and, behold, I will destroy them with the Earth. Genesis 6:13*

> *And, behold, I, even I, do bring a flood of waters upon the Earth, to destroy all flesh, wherein is the breath of life, from under heaven; and every thing that is in the Earth shall die. Genesis 6:17*

So it appears that the Bible gives us two different reasons for sending the disaster:

1. To tempt Job
2. To destroy mankind

I believe, along with major scholars Magee, Schultens, Lowth, and Michaelis that the first parts of the Book of Job were added many centuries after the basic body of the Book had been written. The new writer had not witnessed the disaster as Job had, and did not understand the true context of the Book.

He wrote this front part in an effort to give a reason for the terrible trials to which Job had been subjected.

If this position is accepted, then we have the Bible telling us:

> *And God saw that the wickedness of man was great in the Earth, and that every imagination of the thoughts of his heart was only evil continually. Genesis 6:5*
>
> *And the Lord said, I will destroy man whom I have created from the face of theEarth... Genesis 6:7*

Now, going back to the second oldest written document, the clay tablets of ancient Sumer, we learn that Gilgamesh, the King of ancient Uruk, goes on a mission to seek Utnapishtim, the Sumerian Noah, whom the Gods have made immortal after the flood ordeal.

Utnapishtim tells Gilgamesh why the flood came about:

> **King of Uruk, surely there is no one more bold.**
> **Here is knowledge that no other has ever**

been told.
Near where Euphrates born sits a city you
call Shuruppak, home of those divine.
Enlil sent from there a flood to stop noisy
human babbling all the time.

So the ancient clay tablets of Sumer tell us that the God Enlil caused the flood to stop human noise!

There are several different documented versions of these Biblical and Sumerian reasons for the flood, but all basically say that the Gods caused the flood for one of these two reasons.

There are also many other versions, most of which describe the event, but do not give a reason. Many of these were documented centuries later and may therefore be less accurate.

Perhaps the best example of these is the version documented by Ovid where Phaeton, the son of the god Apollo, drives the chariot of the Sun too close to Earth and sets the world on fire.

So the ancient documents tell us different reasons for the disaster:

1. To tempt Job
2. The wickedness of mankind
3. Mankind making too much noise
4. A God drove the Sun too close to Earth

All of the ancient documentation, however, tell us that God, or a god, caused the flood.

From the scientific evidence, we know that the disaster was caused by a chunk of material from outer space.

It was caused by Satan.

An After-Thought

Concluding that the flood was real, and showing the when, where, and why, is the scope of this book. It would therefore be prudent to stop here.

But the "why" begs further answers - answers that are beyond the scope of this book. That's always the case.

Any answers on any subject always lead to more questions. There's never an end. It's like the commercial that shows the exhausted guy that finally got to the end of the Internet. This, of course, is impossible. One can never have all the answers. There is always another question.

The answers derived from the ancient texts and scientific data leave us hanging from a religious standpoint. And while this is not a book written to answer religious questions, the author feels a need to note that the important question of "why" needs to be better addressed. Many may feel cheated unless there is at least some attempt to address the following questions:

"Did God cause the flood to punish mankind, as stated in the Bible?"

"Surely God didn't cause it because of the noise of mankind as stated in the clay tablets of ancient Sumer?"

Well, we now know that Satan caused the flood.

But Satan was just a big rock. Did God send Satan, or was it just a probability function?

Could it mean that God directs the forces of nature to achieve his actions and will?

The Bible tells us that God sent the flood - and therefore Satan - to destroy most of mankind.

The Bible was written in an ancient era of greater ignorance than yesterday or today. As we gained sophmoric

(Greek for "wise fool") knowledge, we became more agnostic. Some approached athesium and some even became atheists.

But as we continued to gain scientific knowledge, we realized greater truths in the Bible. We began the journey back through agnostism towards the belief in God.

We now know that supernovae explode ever so often and send their debris on paths that eventually impact planets and stars. It's just a matter of time. It is just a probability.

But that does not mean that God had nothing to do with it.

There are atheists that say there is no god; that everything is just a probability function of nature; of physics.

But using their own mathematics, it can easily be shown that the probability of humans coming into existence via natural phenomena is:

> *less than .00000000000000000000001 percent.*

> *Therefore the probability of there being a master creator, a God, is:*
> *99.9999999999999999999 percent.*

Figure 88: God is real.

But, as I said, this is beyond the scope of this book. You can read about it in a forth-coming book: **Humans: How When Why.** Coming soon from:

UnKnownTruths.com
Publishing Company

About the Author

Mr. Parks grew up in the Southern Baptist Tradition and was thus taught the story of Noah and the flood as described in the King James Version of the Bible. Later, while in college, he read the Epic of Gilgamesh as written in the ancient clay tablets of Babylon and Sumer. The stories differed, but were alike in so many ways that it appeared to him that they obviously described the same event.

As the years went by, Mr. Parks continued to hear various versions of the flood story as related by the "myths" from different cultures. It seemed that almost all of the ancient cultures had a version of the flood story. Many of the later cultures also had similar stories, which Mr. Parks assumed had been handed down orally through the ages.

Mr. Parks noticed that all of the stories varied, yet all had some points of similarity.

After he retired from a career as an aerospace engineer and an aerospace executive with a major aerospace company, he decided to study the available information to learn as much as possible about Noah's Flood.

The information discovered presented a troubling dichotomy for Mr. Parks; the scientific evidence did not appear to correlate with his Biblical training. This made Mr. Parks even more interested. He remembered that Jesus had said: "The truth will make you free." John 8:32.

He was determined to find the truth.

Mr. Parks found the truth - the truth that had been unknown down through the ages.

224

This UnKnownTruth inspired the formation of:

UNKNOWNTRUTHS.COM
PUBLISHING COMPANY

And this UnKnownTruth inspired the writing of several books on the subjects of Philosophy and Religion. The first of these books is:

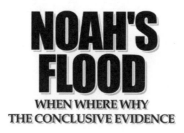

NOAH'S FLOOD

WHEN WHERE WHY
THE CONCLUSIVE EVIDENCE

Walter Hugh Parks

Basic Education

BS Aeronautical Engineering
Mississippi State University
Starkville, Mississippi

MBA
Rollins College
Winter Park, Florida

Post Graduate Work

Astrophysics
UCLA
Los Angeles, California

Laser Physics
University of Michigan
Ann Arbor, Michigan

Informal Education

Mr. Parks has had a life-long hobby of Biblical studies, which in later years have included studies of the Dead Sea Scrolls and many of the ancient clay tablets from Babylon and Sumer.

Mr. Parks also began an intensive study of the human aging process during the last seven years. This has included detailed studies of many of the scientific tests that have been conducted relating to cellular biology, the Human Genome, and Stem Cell Research.

Walter Hugh Parks

Career Experience

1958-1982   Aerospace Engineer with Lockheed
Martin (then Martin Marietta), with
the last six years as Division
General Manager, Tactical
Weapons Systems Division

1982-1986   Co-founder and Chairman of
Parks Jaggers Aerospace Company

1986-1996   Producer, Writer, and Director of
various motion pictures

1997-2002   Writer, Researcher

2003-Present   Founder and President of
UnKnownTruths.com
Publishing Company

Chat Room Participation

Join other readers to discuss your thoughts and criticisms of the book, and to formulate individual and group email for the Publisher and Author.

Chat Room address is:

http://www.unknowntruths.com/discus/
Subject: Noah's Flood

Send emails to:

noahsflood@unknowntruths.com

Order Forms

Additional copies of Noah's Flood, and other books from

**UNKNOWNTRUTHS.COM
PUBLISHING COMPANY**

can be ordered by email or snail mail at the following addresses:

**UNKNOWNTRUTHS.COM
PUBLISHING COMPANY
8815 Conroy Windermere Rd., Ste 190
Orlando, Florida 32835**

Or online at: http://www.unknowntruths.com

Books Available Soon from:

UnKnownTruths.com
Publishing Company

Title	Price
Noah's Flood When Where Why The Conclusive Evidence	$24.95
Immortal Again Methuselah Lived 969 Years Maybe You Can Too!	$24.95
DNA From Atlantis Humans and Food Packages Developments & Migrations Traced	$24.95
So Where Did God Come From The Foundations of Our Religious Beliefs	$24.95
Humans How When Why	$24.95

233

Collectable Artifacts

Collectable Historical Artifacts™ and Collectable Future Artifacts™ are being prepared for the stories of Noah's Flood and forth coming books from:

UNKNOWNTRUTHS.COM PUBLISHING COMPANY

Such collectables from Noah's Flood include various "Rosetta Plaques" suitable for wall decorations, replicas of some of the clay tablets of ancient Sumer and Babylon, and color prints of the encounters of "Satan" with the planets and the Earth. Various paintings of the remains of "Satan" are also available.

The complete listings are available online at:

http://www.unknowntruths.com

Bibliography

A Brief History of Time
Stephen W. Hawking

A History of God
Karen Armstrong

An Analysis of Worlds in Collision
C. Sagan

Ancient Worlds: Peripatetic Geographer from Amasya
Strabo

Atlantis: The Antediluvian World
I. Donnelly

Bode's Law and Missing Planet
M. W. Ovenden

Cataclysm: compelling evidence of a cosmic catastrophe in
D.S. Allan & J.B. Delair

Catastrophic Termination of the Last Wisconsin Ice Advance
C. W. Hunt

Critias
Plato

Deucalion's Flood
Apollodorus

Earth in Upheaval
I. Velikovsky

Enuma Elish: The Babylonian Epic of Creation
S. Langdon

Fossil Mammals and Pollen in a late Pleistocene deposit at
Saltville
B. N. Cooper, C. E. Ray, W. S. Benninghoff

Geography
Strabo

Heaven's Mirror: Quest for the Lost Civilization
Graham Hancock & Santha Faiia

Herodotus Historia
H. Rawlinson

Holy Bible
King James Version

Iliad
Homer

Legendary Islands of the Atlantic
W. H. Babcock

Maps of the Ancient Sea Kings
C. H. Hapgood

On Atlantis
Edgar Cayce

Ovid, P. Metamorphoses
F. J. Miller

Plan of the Pyramid Complex at Giza
John Legon

Pleistocene Volcanism and Glacial Initiation
J. R. Bray

Pliny the Elder Natural History
H. Rackham

Pollen and Diatom-Inferred Climatic and Hydrological
Changes In Sumxi Co Basin (Western Tibet) since 13,000
Years Ago
E. Van Campo, and F. Gasse

Ragnarok: The Age of Fire and Gravel
I. Donnelly

Secret Chamber
Robert Bauval

Serpent in the Sky: The High Wisdom of Ancient Egypt
John West

Sumer: Cities of Eden.
Time-Life Books

The Babylonian Story of the Deluge and the Epic of
Gilgamesh
C. J. Gadd

The Biblical Flood and the Ice Epoch
D. W. Patten

The Bombarded Earth
R. Gallant

The Carolina Bays: are they Meteor Scars?
F. A. & W. Schriever

The Comet of Doom
Rufus Johnson

The Complete Dead Sea Scrolls in English
Geza Vermes

The Greek Myths
R. Graves

The Isaiah Effect: Decoding the Lost Science of Prayer and Prophecy
Gregg Braden

The Legend of Noah
D. C. Allen

The Norse Mythology
R. B. Anderson

The Poetic Edda: Voluspa
H. A. Bellows

When the Sky Fell: In Search of Atlantis
Rand and Rose Flem-Ath

World Mysterie: Sphinx
J.A. West

Numerous Data from the Internet

Photographic/Illustration Credits

Most of our illustrations, while sometimes inspired by material from the various references, are originals. They were created by Dan Diehl.

Some of our illustrations however, are very similar to illustrations in some of the reference materials.

Most of the reference material has been printed and re-printed in various copies and various works down thru the years.

We have obtained proper permissions where needed, although we did not seek permissions from every reference in which the insprational material had been repeated.

We hereby give thanks to the authors of the great body of material which contributed to the research for this book.

Index

A

Andes 84
Andromeda 53
Animal Materials 211
Angra Mainyu 118
Apennines 131
Apollo 122, 124
Apollodorus 148
Appalachia Mountains 213
archeologists 29, 101
archer 123
Arctic 213
Arizona 90, 91
arrow 107, 109
artifacts 2, 28
ashes 114, 129, 131, 190, 194
Asia 214
Assyria 29
Asteroid Belt 69, 70, 109
asteroids 89
astrophysics 226
Athos 129
Atlantian 26, 32
Atlantic Ocean 46, 85, 89
Atlantis 8, 11, 22, 23, 35, 114, 207, 213
atmosphere 41, 43, 46, 80, 85, 90, 94, 167
Australia 214
avalanches 84
Avestic 118
awe 16, 42, 75, 144
awe inspiring 75
Azores 85, 213
Aztecs 94, 161

B

Babylon 17, 121, 100, 224, 226

Babylonian 31, 131
Babylonian Euphrates 131
Babylonians 141
balls of fire 19, 21, 42, 43
barley 145, 199
Bayuan Kara Shan 84
belly 107, 183
Betelgeuse 52, 53
Bible 1, 18, 31, 32, 35, 95, 136, 155, 165, 167, 197, 222-224
Biblical 31, 166, 193, 224
big-headed serpent 54
Bildad 172, 184, 187
bitter cold 96, 160, 161
boats 26
bodies 46, 57, 59, 63, 70, 73, 85, 94, 103, 107, 188
boiled away 82, 85
boiling mud 84
bondage 109
Book of Job 137, 165, 167, 193, 194, 199, 201
Boreas 153
bracelet 109
breast 110, 123, 145
British Isles 213
building chaos 84
bull 13, 123

C

Caicus 131
Cancer 208
captive 109
carbon dating 207
Caribbean 213
Carolina Bays 46, 90
Cascades 84

cubits 103
cuniform 114

D

David 202
debris 40, 45, 51, 70, 73, 80, 82, 83, 85, 89, 90, 94-97, 170, 172, 173, 223
debris clouds 80, 95
debris deposits 89
debris-laden 41, 97
demigods 39
demons 38, 114
depressions 83, 84, 93
destinies 101
destiny 58, 64, 65, 104, 110, 150
destroying 84, 118
destruction 23, 90, 94, 121, 123, 138, 144, 150, 159, 187
Deucalion 32, 35, 148, 152
Devil 37, 137, 156, 201
Dilmun 146
dinosaurs 90
dirt 83, 84
disaster 5, 90, 94, 97, 99, 101, 116, 117, 120, 136, 137, 138, 141, 159, 165, 167, 168, 169, 172, 175, 180, 183, 186, 187, 189, 193, 194, 197, 198, 200, 201, 202, 203, 207
discharges 58, 59, 63, 70, 73, 82, 85, 107, 109
disperse 57, 65
disturbance 23, 59
DNA from Atlantis 233
documentation 99, 143
dolphins 131, 151
Doris 131
downpours 95
dragon 36, 75, 115, 136, 137, 156, 201, 203
drifts 83

dust 40, 83, 84, 85, 167, 168, 172, 184, 190, 194

E

evil 10, 80, 107, 109, 118, 141, 145, 190
Evil One 118
evil wind 80, 107, 109, 145
evolution 3
explode 89, 223
eyewitness 3, 165, 194

F

famine 189
Fenris-Wolf 117
fierce storm winds 107, 109
fiery serpents 43
fire 8, 19, 40, 103, 116-145, 150, 159, 161, 167, 188, 190
firestorms 84
fissures 213
flaming tails 43
float 24
floats 32
flood 1-7, 23, 24, 28-35, 95, 138, 141-148, 152-156, 160,
163, 196, 202, 204, 222, 224, 225
floods 23, 97, 114, 153
Florida 213
flying debris 45
fords 85
fords and locks 85
fossil 213
fountains 31, 129, 131, 155
fractures 213
fragments 29, 101, 117, 138, 145, 159
frightening 75

G

Gaga 104
galaxy 50-53

Ganges 131
Genesis 7, 31, 154-156
genome 226
geological changes 212
giggled 17
glorified 102
Gobi Desert 85
God 7-222
Golden Age 97
Gollveig 116
gopher wood 31, 155
gravel-like stones 90
gravitational field 59
gravitational tidal waves 84, 89
gravity 54, 55, 59, 60, 61, 65, 80
Greek 32, 119, 148, 223
Greeks 141
Greenland 213
grit 80, 84
Gulf of Mexico 90

H

Hades 120
Haemus 129
halo 103
heads 40, 43, 88, 114, 119, 131, 202
heat 39, 43, 46, 82, 84, 90, 93, 95, 96, 107, 125, 127, 131, 134, 138, 159, 161, 171
heaven 8-201
heavenly bodies 46, 70, 94
Hebrews 31
Helicon 129
Herodotus 141
Himalayan Mountains 84
history 5

Judges 79
juniper 145, 189
Jupiter 67, 132, 134

K

kaspu 103
KBO 57
King 7, 8, 11, 14, 17, 22, 29, 32, 35, 39, 101, 120, 144, 145, 146, 150, 179, 181, 189, 202
King Ashurbanipal 29
King James 31, 166
King of Phthia 32, 35
King of Shuruppak 7, 29, 35
King of Uruk 220
kingdom 12
Kingu 70, 75, 88-90, 105, 109, 110, 141
Kronus's 65
Kuiper Belt 56, 57, 59, 103

L

Lahamu 104
Lahmu 104
lakes 82
Lamentations 165
laser physics 226
lava 84, 119
laviathan 2, 3, 5, 32, 45, 46, 75, 94, 95
Libyan Desert 131
lightning 134, 150, 198
lion 123, 152
locks 149
Lord 31, 105, 107, 120, 137, 149, 155, 161, 165, 167, 203
Lugalbanda 198, 199

M

magma 84
magnetic field 63, 73
mankind 5, 7, 28-31, 79, 113, 144-150, 166, 222
Marduk 16-19, 80, 90, 101-113
maritime 32
Mark Twain 99
Mars 70, 72, 73, 104
mass 54, 55, 57, 59, 63, 69, 70, 75, 77, 87, 89, 91
mathematics 223
Meander 131
memories 97, 141
Merlota 11
Meru 26, 39, 114
mesmerized 43
Mesopotamia 17, 142
Mesopotamians 16, 80
Metamorphoses 122, 237
meteors 89
Michael 136, 156, 201
migrations 233
Milky Way Galaxy 51, 53
Mim 116
Mindanao Islands 214
miserable 172, 177, 183
moisture 43
monster 81, 115, 119
monsters 123
Mont Aetna 119
moon 59, 65, 69, 70, 75, 64, 91, 94, 101, 104, 105, 109,
125, 129, 136, 141, 187, 200
moons 59, 62, 63, 65, 72, 73
Mount Meru 26, 39
mountains 24, 26, 39, 84, 92, 93, 115, 117, 119, 129, 131,
136, 138, 145, 146, 148, 159, 173, 198, 200, 211, 213

mudslides 84
multi-headed serpent 74
Muses 129
Myth 1, 4, 32
myths 2, 5, 32, 75

N

Naiads 130, 134
natural phenomena 223
nebula 51
necklace 18, 19
Neptune 8, 10, 17, 58, 59, 60, 61, 63, 65, 67, 104, 131
Nereid 59, 131
Nereids 131
Nereus 131
Nile 131
Nimrod 17, 19
Ninevah 29
Noah 1, 4, 7, 30, 32, 35, 155
noise 45, 81, 82, 144, 147, 221, 222
Norse 116, 117, 141, 160, 238
North Atlantic 213
North Atlantic Ocean 85
North Sea 213
Norway 210-213
nuclear 51
Nymphs of Corycus 152

O

Oceania 214
OEte 129
Olympus 120, 131
Oracles 152
orbit 57, 59-70, 75, 89, 91, 103, 105, 109, 110, 215

priest 8, 17, 25, 32, 35, 144, 148, 165, 168, 179, 180, 181, 182
probability 222, 223
Prometheus 32, 148
Psalms 202
pulsar 51, 53
pyramids 53

Q

Queen of Heaven 17, 19

R

Ra 11
radiated 95, 96
rain 31, 84, 93, 95, 96, 148, 153, 154, 155, 160, 167, 188, 193
records 22, 101, 121, 213, 215
red hot 8, 43
redeposit 80
reed wall 28
reins 123, 125, 127, 129
religious beliefs 233
remnant 48, 50, 51
Revelation 37, 136, 156, 200
reverberating aftershocks 85
Rhodope 129
Rigveda 114
rivers 82, 85, 131, 202
Roche Zone 88, 89
Rockies 85
Rome's Metamorphoses 122
Rosetta Plaques 235
rotational equilibrium 73
rules 43, 116

Russian 94, 160

S

saber-tooth tiger 215
sacred bull 13
Satan 6-210
Saturn 65, 64, 67, 104
Scandinavian 85
scholars 29, 165, 167, 168, 193, 220
science 5, 65, 69, 238
scientific evidence 49, 166, 168, 205, 221, 224
scorpion 123, 129
Scythia 131
sea animals 93
sea nymphs 151
seal 110, 136, 200
seismic activity 85
Semiramis 16, 17, 19
serpent 10, 37, 39, 46, 55, 57, 70, 75, 113-118, 127, 137, 141, 156, 188, 201, 203
serpents 43-45
Set 58, 104, 118, 125, 126, 150, 170, 187
shelters 82, 181
shifted 85
ships 24
shock waves 44, 46
shooting stars 21, 43
Shuruppak 29, 35, 221
Siberian mammoths 207
sinking 84, 213
Sisera 79
smoke 84, 85, 94, 119, 129, 131, 170, 172, 173
snow 96, 118, 160, 193
solar system 51, 55, 56, 57, 59, 67, 69, 70, 103, 104
South Carolina 46

speed of light 55
spewing rocks 84
spiral 70
spirit 170, 172, 188
spit fire 43
spitting fire 8
steam 82, 84, 116
steamed 82
steeds 125, 127
stem cell research 226
Strabo 141
Sumer 69, 100, 101, 113, 121, 220, 222, 224, 226
Sumerian 29, 31, 101, 144, 198, 220
sun 11, 14, 21, 39, 43, 55, 57-70, 77, 93, 94, 97, 101, 105, 109, 113, 116-118
supernova 48-55, 67, 77, 103, 167
Surt 116
swallowing 85
swarm 46, 57, 59, 82, 188, 202
swirling debris 82

T

Tagus 131
tail 43, 57, 54, 109, 129
Tammuz 17
Tanais 131
Tartarus 131
Taurus 129
Ta-Wats 21, 35, 42, 43, 44, 138, 159
tectonic plates 84
tempest 80, 129, 174, 178
Tethys 122
The Epic of Creation 101
Themis 120, 152
theologians 49

U

V

valleys 83, 138, 159, 189
Vela 51, 103
Vela Supernova Remnant 48, 51
Venus 104
violating 43
volcanoes 84, 94, 97
Vritra 114, 115
Vulcan 124, 150

W

war in heaven 37, 49, 75, 98, 99, 136, 156, 160, 201
warning 7, 22, 23, 24, 26, 29, 31, 32, 35, 43, 82
water vapor 85, 94, 95, 97
waves 24, 46, 87, 92, 93, 95, 131, 151, 152, 153, 173, 181
whales 93
whip 125
whirlwind 80
whistle 81
wind 40, 43, 45, 80, 105, 107, 109, 167, 168, 183
wolfe 151
womb 107, 193
wooly mammoth 215
Wrong Way Orbit 67

X

Xanthus 131

Y

Yggdrasil 116
Yima 118, 161
Yucatan Peninsular 90

Z

Zeus 119, 120, 132, 148, 150
Ziggurat 16
Ziusudra 7, 28, 29, 31, 35, 143, 144
zodiac 129
zodiacal constellation of Cancer 208
Zophas 177